THE TRAUMA AND
ATTACHMENT-AWARE CLASSROOM

THE TRAUMA AND ATTACHMENT-AWARE CLASSROOM

A Practical Guide to Supporting Children Who Have Encountered Trauma and Adverse Childhood Experiences

Rebecca Brooks

Jessica Kingsley *Publishers*
London and Philadelphia

First published in 2020
by Jessica Kingsley Publishers
73 Collier Street
London N1 9BE, UK
and
400 Market Street, Suite 400
Philadelphia, PA 19106, USA

www.jkp.com

Library of Congress Cataloging in Publication Data
A CIP catalog record for this book is available from the Library of Congress

British Library Cataloguing in Publication Data
A CIP catalogue record for this book is available from the British Library

ISBN 978 1 78592 558 0
eISBN 978 1 78592 877 2

Printed and bound in Great Britain

Acknowledgements

With heartfelt thanks to the many parents, guardians, children and educators whose insights have added such value to this book, and especially to Benjamin Adlard Primary School, Burnside Primary School, Bury Church of England High School, Cheadle Primary School, Colebourne Primary School and The de Ferrers Academy.

Contents

A Note About the UK Education System

In the UK, education is a devolved matter, with each nation's administration governing its own education provision. As a result, the curriculum, examinations, funding streams and inspection regimes are different across the UK.

Here is a short guide to some of the terms and concepts included in this volume which may be unfamiliar to some readers:

Year groups, ages and stages

England and Wales

Compulsory education begins at age five, but in practice, children usually begin their education during the school year after their fourth birthday, and continue until they are 16. In England young people over 16 must be engaged in full- or part-time education or an apprenticeship or traineeship until they are 18.

The school system is divided into stages. The Early Years Foundation Stage (EYFS) covers children aged three to five, including the first year of primary school (Reception). Key Stage 1 covers children aged five to seven (Years 1 and 2). Key Stage 2 covers children aged 7 to 11 (Years 3–6). At secondary school, Key Stage 3 includes children aged 11 to 14 (Years 7–9), Key Stage 4 covers young people aged 14 to 16 (Years 10–11) and Key Stage 5 covers young people aged 16 to 18 (Years 12–13).

A small number of areas operate a middle school system, where children will transfer from primary to middle school at Year 5 or 6, and remain there for approximately three years before moving on to secondary or upper school.

Scotland

Children begin their compulsory education aged between four and a half and five and a half, depending on when their birthday falls. They remain at primary school for seven years (P1–P7) and, aged 11 or 12, move to secondary school for four years (S1–S4), with an optional further two years (S5–S6).

Northern Ireland

Children usually start school in the September after their fourth birthday, and attend until they are 16. The schools system is divided into stages, comprising Foundation Stage for children aged four to six (P1–P2), Key Stage 1 for children aged six to eight (P3–P4) and Key Stage 2 for children aged 8 to 11 (P5–P7) at primary school. At secondary school, Key Stage 3 covers children aged 11 to 14 (Years 8–10) and Key Stage 4 covers young people aged 14 to 16 (Years 11–12).

Statutory examinations

Across the UK, students will take statutory examinations towards the end of their compulsory schooling at or around age 16. In England, Wales and Northern Ireland, students will take General Certificate of Secondary Education (GCSE) examinations in several subjects. Those who continue post-16 can study AS-Levels followed by A-Levels, or a range of other more vocational qualifications.

In Scotland, students can take National 3/4/5 at or around age 16, and then go on to take Highers and Advanced Highers as part of their further, non-compulsory education.

Each nation has its own arrangements for monitoring student progress throughout their education. For example, in England, all children also undergo a formal statutory assessment at the end of Key Stage 1 and Key Stage 2 in the core subjects of English Language (including reading and writing), Mathematics and Science. These assessments are commonly called SATs and are a combination of teacher assessments and formal tests.

Special or additional educational needs

In each nation of the UK, there is a system for providing children with complex special or additional needs or disabilities with a legal document which details their needs, and the support that will be offered to them. In England this is called the Education, Health and Care Plan (EHCP); in Wales it is the Individual Development Plan (IDP); in Northern Ireland it is the Statement of Special Educational Needs; in Scotland it is the Co-ordinated Support Plan (CSP).

Introduction

It is nearly 20 years now since a Romanian charity worker gave me a crash course in attachment and trauma. I was volunteering at a summer camp in north-eastern Romania. All of the girls at the camp lived in Romania's institutions – orphanages, as we came to call them in the West – and the charity I was volunteering for organised annual holidays for them, amongst other activities.

My Romanian friend's run-down of what we could expect from these girls and young women sounded a little harsh to my naive ears. We were warned that they might indiscriminately attach to us, seek close physical affection even though they barely knew our names, and hang around at the end of the camp, hoping to be given gifts of spare toiletries, trinkets and clothes as we packed up our things.

'They will make you feel as if you're so special to them,' she said, 'but you're just another group of people in their lives who are here today, gone tomorrow. It's all about survival.'

The very next evening, a nine-year-old girl attempted to sit on my lap and cuddle up to me like a toddler while we were watching a film. In fact, everything we had been told was accurate. These girls were as varied as any group of children and teens you might find – variously funny, smart, boisterous, timid, sporty, bookish – but they were all survivors of Romania's infamous orphanage system, abandoned to the state for various reasons, and subject to a carousel of paid carers and volunteers in institutions that could house hundreds of children. The impact was obvious in the way they approached every aspect of their lives.

I didn't immediately make the connection between the challenges faced by these young women, and those faced by many children I encountered in the classroom. However, many more summer camps, two years spent living and working with Romania's *copii abandonați*, and my own experiences as both a foster carer and an adoptive parent have demonstrated to me beyond doubt that childhood trauma can have a devastating impact on the development and life chances of children.

This is a view that is increasingly borne out by research and statistical evidence, and there are few places where this impact is more keenly felt than in our schools. Children who have experienced the worst possible start in life are routinely struggling, failing and being excluded from school. They are more likely to have special educational needs, more likely to be excluded, and more likely to leave school without any qualifications. The challenges they face in school spill over to bring chaos to home lives, and impact on the students and teachers who share the classroom with them.

When I made that first visit to Romania, I had already been trained as a teacher and spent years in various secondary school classrooms, and yet I had never even heard of attachment disorder, or Foetal Alcohol Spectrum Disorders, or many of the other difficulties experienced by children who have had adverse childhood experiences. As my understanding grew, I couldn't help but think of some of the children who had been through my classrooms in a new light, and wonder whether I could have done things differently for them if I had known and understood the complexity that lay behind their difficulties.

What follows is the book I wish I had when I was in the classroom every day, faced with class after class of children and young people, breathtaking in their variety, complexity and individuality. There are some explanations, some descriptions and some tried-and-tested strategies, as well as contributions from parents and carers of traumatised children, and from several schools which have embarked on a journey towards a more attachment- and trauma-informed approach.

It is my hope that within these pages you will find something that will equip and empower you to support the student you had in mind when you picked up this book, because I believe wholeheartedly that, as an educator, you have the ability to powerfully transform the lives of the young people you will encounter.

Chapter 1

THE IMPACT OF EARLY TRAUMA

In this chapter:

Trauma, attachment and the developing child

When attachments are insecure

Toxic stress

Toxic shame

Beyond attachment

How much attention do you pay to the foundations of your house? The chances are you rarely give them much thought. They are just there, doing their job (we hope). It is only when problems appear with the visible part of the structure that you might start to give serious consideration to what lies beneath. A huge crack suddenly appearing in a load-bearing wall will quickly spur a householder to investigate further.

In many ways, the development that takes place in a child before birth, and during infancy and early childhood is very much like the foundations of a house. It is not remembered and not often thought about, but these foundations form the basis on which a child's later experiences, learning and development will be built. If they are unstable, the whole building will be affected.

Repeated traumatic experiences in childhood can have a devastating impact on the stability of the foundations of a child's development. Dr Bruce Perry of the US-based Child Trauma Academy, defines psychological trauma as 'an experience, or pattern of experiences, that impairs the proper functioning of the person's stress-response system, making it more reactive

quote

or sensitive' (Supin, 2016). Traumatic events threaten our own life or physical safety, or that of those around us for whom we care, have empathy or responsibility. They are overwhelming events. An acute traumatic event might be a serious accident, a natural disaster, a sudden or violent loss of a loved one, or an assault.

Complex trauma occurs when a person is exposed to multiple traumatic events, or many repetitions of a similar trauma, such as physical, sexual or emotional abuse, or domestic violence. In these situations, the effects of chronic trauma can be cumulative as each traumatic event acts as a triggering reminder to previous events.

It is not difficult for us to imagine events that would be classed as traumatic. We may have experienced them ourselves, and we are likely to be able to understand and empathise with traumatic experiences faced by some children. If we consider a child of seven or eight years old witnessing domestic violence on a regular basis, for instance, it is easy to understand that this is traumatic and those around the child are likely to respond sensitively and empathetically.

Empathising with trauma experienced by an infant or very young child is perhaps not so straightforward. It is tempting to imagine that children so young can have no real experience of trauma or that, since it is not consciously remembered, it will have no lasting effect. Yet, to a tiny infant, dependent for their very existence on their caregiver, being left alone, hungry and crying for long periods is truly a threat to their physical safety and even to their life – a traumatic event. Events that constitute trauma for a very young child might look a little different from those an adult would consider traumatic, but their impact is no less. Although the conscious memory may not record these events, the title of Dr Bessel van der Kolk's best-selling book reminds us that *The Body Keeps the Score* (van der Kolk, 2014).

Trauma, attachment and the developing child

Our understanding of the human brain is still far from complete, but the evidence so far suggests three things that are vital to our understanding of how early trauma and adverse experiences can affect its development:

1. Many of the brain's basic systems involved in, for instance, managing stress or regulating emotional arousal are not fully formed at birth and will continue to be developed during the first two years of life.

2. The development of the human brain happens stage by stage, from primitive reflexes up to higher-order language and thinking skills, and each of these stages is foundational to the next. In short, if something goes wrong at any stage, all the developmental stages afterwards could be affected.

3. This development is highly dependent on the social environment surrounding an infant. The brain learns and develops according to its experiences, creating networks of neurons where needed, and pruning away what is not needed. The brains of infants and toddlers are highly adaptable and plastic.

Even before a baby is born, the development of their brain is well underway. A whole host of bio-chemical signals from the mother begin to prepare the developing foetus for the environment that they can expect once they are born. As early as the first trimester of pregnancy, the first neurons and synapses begin to develop in the brain, allowing the foetus to make its first tiny movements. The sensory feedback from these movements will spur on more development. In the second trimester, the synapses of the cerebral cortex begin to develop, and the process of myelination begins, allowing for faster processing of information.

Prolonged or severe maternal stress during pregnancy can cause the stress hormone cortisol to cross the placenta, affecting the development of the amygdala (Gerhardt, 2014). Maternal alcohol and drug use can also have devastating impacts. Alcohol is a teratogen which can cross the placenta and have a range of effects on the developing foetus, depending on the stage of the pregnancy. Pre-natal alcohol exposure is considered to be a leading preventable cause of birth defects and neurodevelopmental disorders (Guerri *et al.*, 2009). We will look in more detail at the impact of alcohol in the next chapter.

Once born, an infant is wholly dependent on their primary caregiver for their survival. With no mechanism for understanding the sensations in their bodies, or contextualising their experiences, every crisis is, as far as they are concerned, a life-threatening one. From their first days, newborn infants are primed to prioritise the relationship that is most likely to ensure their survival – the relationship with their mother, whose voice, smell and heartbeat they have become so familiar with during the months of pregnancy. A newborn baby can recognise human faces and prefers them to other objects. Their field of vision extends just as far as the face of the person who is holding them. They signal their urgent distress with cries, and reward our attentions with tiny grips of their fingers and, very soon, endearing smiles and noises.

Slowly, over the first few weeks, the baby begins to make sense of the world. Day and night begin to separate, different faces come to have meaning, and the baby begins to form expectations about the world around them. What the baby cannot yet do is to recognise their sensations and emotional states, and neither can they do anything about them. It is the role of adults to attend to these things. Above all, infants need caregivers who are responsive to their needs, who are attuned to them, and available for them. Rees (2017, p.23) describes attunement as a parent's ability 'to see into their child's mind'. In a well-attuned relationship, a parent or caregiver will, most of the time, interpret the child's cries, sounds, facial expressions and body language and respond appropriately. Through regular interactions, which are sometimes called 'serve and return' interactions, even a tiny infant will begin to learn at a basic level that they are safe, their needs will be met, and the world is essentially a good place to be.

Take the hungry infant. Unable to differentiate between his feelings, all he knows is unpleasant and frightening sensations and all he can do is cry about it. His caregiver responds to his intense distress, perhaps mirroring his discomfort with their facial expression and tone, and then using a soothing voice as they prepare to feed him. As he feeds, the baby's stress subsides, the cortisol flooding his body melts away, and he can return to a relaxed state, knowing his need has been met. This is the attachment cycle in action, and it is repeated many times during every day. Over time the baby will learn to regulate his own emotions from the example he has been shown thousands of times throughout his infancy. Without consciously realising it, the baby begins to absorb patterns of behaviour, expectations of how the world works, based on the serve and return interactions he experiences.

As the baby grows and develops into a toddler, these subconscious expectations will form the foundation for the next stage of his development. The attachment cycle for a toddler is increasingly about exploration from a safe base. Think about taking a young toddler to, say, a doctor's surgery waiting room. At first, they might sit on your knee, needing the security of feeling you close by while they assess their environment. Gradually they become bolder, getting down and even wandering a few steps away to explore the magazines and toys. Then a stranger walks into the waiting room. This turns what has been a safe situation into a potentially stressful one, and the toddler returns to your side, seeking once again the safety and security of your immediate presence. If the stranger proves to be no kind of threat, then the toddler might begin to explore again, and so the cycle goes on. As the child grows older, their exploration will take them in wider and wider circles from the safe base of their caregiver until they are ready to be separated for long periods, knowing for certain that their safe base will be there at the end of the day.

During these first vital months and years, the brain is developing at speed, and this development relies, in large part, on the experiences the child will have. The newborn comes ready with the core parts of the brain that will regulate autonomic functions like breathing and digesting, and soon after will come the ability to respond to external stimulus, either by turning towards it or freezing or flinching away from it. The amygdala, which detects threat and responds to it, is developing throughout early childhood in accordance with the environment the child experiences. Similarly, the cortex – what is sometimes called the 'thinking' part of the brain – takes years to develop through play and touch and interaction.

When a child hears speech sounds, for instance, synapses between neurons in the language-related parts of the brain are stimulated. The more speech an infant hears, the more stimulation takes place, and the stronger the synapses become. By the end of a child's first year, their brain will be wired for the language they hear at home. A baby's brain will double in weight during the first year of life. It has more synapses than it will ever need, making it highly adaptable to its environment but, from toddlerhood onwards, weak, rarely used synapses begin to be pruned away. The context within which all this rapid and foundational development will take place is that of the earliest and most vital attachment relationships that a child has.

When attachments are insecure

The majority of children will develop secure attachments with their primary caregivers through 'good enough' parenting that is attuned to their needs most of the time and responds appropriately. Occasional lapses will not derail the growing attachment. However, sometimes this developing attachment relationship can be disrupted, often by circumstances outside of anybody's control. With the best will in the world, if a baby has to spend many weeks in hospital, the development of the attachment relationship can be inhibited. If there is post-natal depression, or a crisis in the family home, or the family is in a chronically difficult situation, it may not be possible for the primary caregiver to be as attentive and attuned as they would want to be. Sadly in some cases, it is abusive or neglectful parenting that derails the attachment cycle.

A US-based longitudinal study has revealed that about 40 per cent of children are insecurely attached (Andreassen and West, 2007). Attachment theorists have differentiated varying attachment 'styles' (Ainsworth and Bell, 1970; Main and Solomon, 1990) to describe the outworking of a child's insecure attachment with their primary caregiver but, essentially, children's main responses are to either minimise expressions of need – avoid their caregiver, and make themselves small, invisible or compliant – or to exaggerate their expressions of need to try to engage their caregiver. Some children who simply cannot learn a coherent way to manage their distress are said to exhibit 'disorganised attachment'.

It is tempting to see these attachment styles as neat labels to attach to children, but they are not as simple as that. The styles of attachment as described by attachment theorists relate to the child's attachment relationship with their primary caregiver. They are not set in stone for a child's whole life. A child may respond differently to different attachment figures in their lives and at different times in their development. What is important is that the child's ability to learn how relationships work, to regulate themselves, and to develop healthy independence from a secure base is derailed when their primary attachment relationship is insecure. These effects are not a choice made by the child, but a result of their developing brain's adaptation to the environment in which they are being raised.

Insecure early attachments lead to increased risk for problems such as anxiety, aggression and hyper-activity, which can occur regardless of socio-economic status (Fearon et al., 2010). Attachment has been shown to influence children's early language development (Belsky and Fearon, 2002), the development of their executive function, and their ability to respond flexibly to new ideas and demands (Bernier et al., 2012). Insecurely attached children are more likely to have behavioural difficulties at school, more likely to be bullies or be bullied, and less likely to be curious, self-confident and resilient (Tough, 2012).

Toxic stress

Everybody will experience stress in their lives, including small children. Learning to cope with stress is part of life, and an important part of child development. When we feel threatened, our bodies prepare for fight, flight or freeze by raising our heart rate and blood pressure, and releasing stress hormones such as cortisol. We have seen how, as part of a healthy attachment cycle, infant stress is routinely soothed by the primary caregiver, allowing the child's body to return to a normal state. Over time this allows the child to develop healthy stress response systems. Even children who experience serious hardship can still develop 'resilience' if they have the buffer of a strong, supportive attachment relationship.

However, if the stress is extreme and long-lasting, and is not buffered by a secure attachment relationship, healthy stress response systems may not develop. Resilience is built in a child. It is not an innate trait of all children. Research into the prevalence of adverse childhood experiences (ACEs) has shown a link between toxic stress in childhood and a range of developmental and health problems later in life, including increased risk of diabetes, heart disease, substance abuse and depression (Felitti *et al.*, 1998). If a child is not able to develop healthy stress response systems, then they are less resilient to future stress, however slight that stress might seem to an onlooker. A child who has experienced toxic stress may be operating at a higher general level of stress than others, and have a strong fight–flight–freeze reaction to such everyday occurrences as someone entering the room unexpectedly, an unusual sound in the classroom, or a minor change to the usual routine.

The impact of stress can begin before a child is born. High levels of maternal cortisol during the third trimester of pregnancy have been linked to lower verbal IQ scores in the child (LeWinn *et al.*, 2009). Once born, infants tend to have low baseline levels of cortisol, but can quickly spike their levels if nobody is responding to their cries. Throughout early childhood a child will begin to establish the 'normal' pattern of high cortisol in the morning and lower cortisol later in the day. However, if high cortisol levels are left to persist in an infant, such as in a stressful situation with no secure attachment relationship to buffer the stress, over time, the structures of the brain that manage stress can become weakened. Toxic stress overloads the stress management systems. The result can be either children who maintain persistently high cortisol levels, and react dramatically to the slightest stressor, or children with unusually low baseline cortisol levels, who don't seem to react much to anything at all (Gerhardt, 2014).

The research on the impact of toxic stress is still developing but although we do not yet fully understand the processes at work, it seems that prolonged, severe stress in early childhood, without the buffer of a secure attachment relationship, can have long-term damaging effects. There will be many children in our classrooms who are apparently over-reacting to the slightest thing as a result of poor stress response systems caused by toxic stress. There will be many others whose defence against stress is to essentially flatline their emotional responses. It is important that educators are able to recognise and respond to both.

Toxic shame

As with stress, shame is a feeling that we will all experience, and developing healthy responses to appropriate feelings of shame and guilt should be part of life for us all. However, just as our stress response systems are developed within the context of our early attachment relationships, so also is our system for dealing with shame and guilt. Within any relationship, there will be occasions where there is a temporary breakdown. Maybe the exhausted parent does not hear the baby cry in the small hours of the morning, or the toddler becomes distressed on being firmly told 'No!' It is not possible for any parent to be completely attuned at all times and, sometimes, toddlers do need to be told 'No', even if it does make them cry.

In a healthy attachment relationship, these small ruptures will quickly be repaired. The exhausted parent will startle awake and then go to their crying infant to soothe them. The securely attached toddler will likely seek comfort for their distress at being reprimanded, and will accept cuddles and calming words. It's what Dr Daniel Siegel (1999, p.116) calls 'rupture and repair', and its repetition many times throughout childhood helps children to develop a healthy approach to managing their own feelings of shame or guilt, as they see adults model the 'repair' part of the cycle and learn that these hard feelings do eventually fade away.

But what if the repair never comes? When a child's needs are consistently unmet within their attachment relationship – whether those needs are physical or emotional – they learn that their needs don't matter and, eventually, that they themselves don't matter. When relationships are ruptured through rough words, shouting, even physical violence, and not repaired, the child is left drowning in the strong feelings of their shame, with no way out. If the adult doesn't make it right again, then the child cannot recover.

It has been said that the difference between guilt and shame is that guilt says, 'I did something bad', whereas shame says, 'I am bad.' For children who have been in care, an inner view of themselves and their needs as worthless and shameful, caused by insecure early attachments, neglect and abuse, is only compounded by the loss of their birth families, and any subsequent moves through the care system.

This has implications for how we manage children's behaviour in school. For children who already believe themselves to be 'bad', any attempt to impress on them the 'badness' of what they have done only confirms their inner view of themselves. They already feel as bad about themselves as it is possible to feel, so attempts to correct behaviour that shame them, publicly criticise them or compare them unfavourably to others only heighten intolerable feelings of worthlessness and shame which must be defended against at all costs. For this reason, some children will do anything, say anything, rather than make an admission, even when the evidence is incontrovertible. Their self-protection may manifest as a defensive rage, turning the tables on their accuser with angry words and actions. Alternatively, they may retreat into themselves, ignoring the authority figure and shutting down emotionally. It is not anger or defiance that is at the root of such behaviour, but deep, deep shame.

Beyond attachment

Attachment is important, and we have seen that insecure early attachments affect a large proportion of people, with long-lasting and appreciable consequences. However, the relational trauma experienced as a result of unmet attachment needs is just one thread of the tapestry of trauma that has been experienced by many children who have been removed from their families and placed with long-term foster carers, adoptive parents, family members or special guardians. Relationships are at the heart of infant development, so the impact of other traumatic experiences will always be seen in the context of children's early attachment experiences, but it is vital that we look beyond basic attachment theory when supporting children with a history of complex trauma. In the next chapter, we will consider a broader range of difficulties that are often faced by children who have experienced a traumatic start in life.

> I very much regret not finding a school that would support social and emotional development more, because it really is the only thing that counts towards my daughter's future mental health and happiness. I feel like I am watching helplessly as my daughter veers along towards adolescent mental health problems which could be prevented if the best actions could be taken now.

Chapter 2

DIAGNOSES AND DIFFICULTIES

In this chapter:

Developmental Trauma Disorder

Complex Post Traumatic Stress Disorder

Attachment difficulties and disorders

Foetal Alcohol Spectrum Disorders

Pathological Demand Avoidance

Speech, language and communication

Sensory processing difficulties

Executive functioning difficulties

Physical development

Special educational needs

Children with complex trauma histories may arrive at school with a smorgasbord of overlapping diagnoses and disorders. Others will have no official diagnosis. There are many factors which can make it difficult to get appropriate diagnoses for children who have experienced complex trauma, not least the fact that vital information about the child's early experiences might not be known to the carers and professionals involved in their care, especially if the child has been removed from their birth family and is living permanently elsewhere.

Challenges faced by children with complex needs are often overlapping – for instance, the Coventry Grid (Moran, 2010) details the significant overlaps between attachment difficulties and autistic spectrum disorder. It can be difficult to unpick the complex tapestry of needs and challenges faced by some children, some of which will only become apparent as the child matures, milestones are missed, and any differences between them and their peers widen.

While diagnoses and descriptions of specific difficulties are often necessary, and we will detail several of the most relevant examples here, it is vitally important to remember that a child-centred approach will always put the presenting needs of the child first, rather than the diagnosis first. The support a child needs at any given time will depend on a number of factors, including historical and current circumstances, so support should not begin and end with a diagnosis.

Developmental Trauma Disorder

Coined by Dr Bessel van der Kolk, Developmental Trauma Disorder aims to be a catch-all diagnosis that encompasses the various challenges that may be faced by those who have experienced repeated or chronic childhood trauma. Van der Kolk and his colleagues at the Trauma Centre of the Justice Resource Institute in the US campaigned to have Developmental Trauma Disorder included in the American Psychiatric Association's *Diagnostic and Statistical Manual of Mental Disorders 5* (*DSM-5*), because it was felt that none of the existing diagnoses available properly capture the complexity of the impact of chronic trauma, leading to people being misdiagnosed, or diagnosed with a plethora of overlapping conditions. Despite the *DSM-5* not including the diagnosis in its final version (which has been called 'a missed opportunity' (Bremness and Polzin, 2014)), the terms 'developmental trauma' and 'developmental trauma disorder' are now increasingly being used among professionals treating attachment and trauma disorders in children both in the US and the UK.

Developmental Trauma Disorder encompasses both the physiological and psychological difficulties that can arise from complex early trauma, including inability to regulate stress responses, hyper-vigilance, risk-taking behaviours, inappropriate self-soothing behaviours, diminished awareness of bodily sensations and states, sensory difficulties, attention difficulties, executive functioning difficulties, tendency to physical and verbal aggression, and pervasive negative self-image.

Complex Post Traumatic Stress Disorder

Complex Post Traumatic Stress Disorder (Complex PTSD) is a diagnosis recognised by the NHS in the UK that covers the range of difficulties that can arise as a result of complex early trauma. There are overlaps between Complex PTSD and Post Traumatic Stress Disorder (PTSD), and some children are diagnosed with PTSD, but Complex PTSD, like Developmental Trauma Disorder, aims to capture the full picture of challenges faced by those who have experienced multiple or chronic traumatic events in early childhood, unlike PTSD, which is more associated with single traumatic events, or individual periods of traumatic events.

The NHS description of the symptoms of Complex PTSD includes difficulty controlling emotions, dissociation, physical symptoms such as headaches, dizziness and stomach aches, relationship difficulties, and destructive or risky behaviour (NHS Choices, 2018). Treating Complex PTSD will require a multi-disciplinary approach, and often involve a combination of therapies.

Attachment difficulties and disorders

As we have seen in Chapter 1, insecure early attachment relationships can have a profound and lasting impact on a child as they grow. The NICE guidance on Children's Attachment (2015) uses the term 'attachment difficulties' to include both diagnosed attachment disorders and more general difficulties around forming secure attachments. While many children who have experienced disrupted and insecure early attachments will exhibit attachment difficulties (attachment to their caregiver is described as avoidant, ambivalent or disorganised), only two disorders are defined in the *DSM* (American Psychiatric Association, 2013) and International Classification of Diseases (*ICD*) (World Health Organisation, 2018) classifications: Reactive Attachment Disorder, and Disinhibited Attachment Disorder (also called Disinhibited Social Engagement Disorder).

Reactive Attachment Disorder (RAD) is described by NICE (2015) as 'a consistent and pervasive pattern of behaviour in which a child shows extremely withdrawn behaviour, particularly a marked tendency to not show attachment behaviour towards caregivers…accompanied by a general lack of responsiveness to others'. A child with RAD will have a very negative view of themselves, and may also experience 'marked sadness, fearfulness or irritability'.

Children with Disinhibited Attachment Disorder (DAD) lack caution around unfamiliar adults, and are insensitive to social boundaries. They may willingly go off with strangers, act as if their caregiver isn't there even in unfamiliar places and situations, and display over-familiar behaviour towards strangers. Both of these diagnoses require a known history of very insufficient care, and the patterns of behaviour must have begun while a child was young, and be consistent.

Although as many as 40 per cent of people may have insecure attachments, the majority of them will not be diagnosed with one of the conditions described above. Some children may be described as having 'attachment problems', and as many as 80 per cent of children who have been abused or neglected may exhibit 'disorganised attachment behaviour' (NICE, 2015) although this in itself is not a diagnosis.

Attachment problems can have a significant impact on a child's school life. Children spend hours each day with teachers and other members of staff, forming relationships that have some level of attachment to them, and these successful relationships impact positively on a child's wellbeing and engagement with learning. Children and young people with better emotional and social wellbeing are likely to achieve more academically, make more progress in primary school and be more engaged in secondary school (Brooks, 2014; Gutman and Vorhaus, 2012). Children who struggle to form relationships with their teachers and peers are missing out on this important driver towards educational success.

Difficulties such as poor self-regulation and low self-esteem will impact negatively on a child's ability to learn and make progress. If a child's internal view of themselves is that they are bad and worthless, then their persistence in the face of difficult tasks will be very low. Some children will engage in 'attention-seeking' (really 'attachment-seeking') behaviour which can include constantly trying to attract a teacher's attention by clinginess, incessant chatter and noise, and disruptive behaviour. Others may hide from relationships with teachers, masking their difficulties, never putting up their hands, and not seeking comfort when threatened or hurt. Children with attachment difficulties who appear 'fine' and 'settled' at school may well be in turmoil under the surface and experiencing considerable distress which may manifest itself elsewhere as meltdowns and aggressive behaviours, or be internalised as self-harm, anxiety and depression. NICE (2015) places emphasis on the fact that 'Adopted children with attachment difficulties can have further difficulties in many aspects of daily life...and their behaviour needs to be fully understood by their adoptive parents, educators and supporters.'

Foetal Alcohol Spectrum Disorders

Foetal Alcohol Spectrum Disorders (FASD) is an umbrella term for disabilities that result from pre-natal alcohol exposure. These disabilities can have profound physical and neurological effects that are lifelong. Alcohol in the mother's bloodstream can pass through the placenta to the developing baby at any time during the pregnancy, even before the mother knows she is pregnant. It can cause a number of physical malformations as well as learning and behavioural difficulties, meaning that children who are diagnosed with one of the conditions under the FASD umbrella can exhibit a range of symptoms in varying degrees of severity. In the UK, there are four diagnoses under the FASD umbrella:

- Foetal Alcohol Syndrome (FAS): Children with FAS are often recognisable because of their distinctive facial abnormalities (small eyes, thin upper lip, small head, no philtrum). Other symptoms include movement and co-ordination problems, difficulties with speech, executive function, memory and handling numbers, mood and behavioural problems, small stature and poor growth, and physical problems with organs such as the liver, kidneys and heart.

- Partial Foetal Alcohol Syndrome (PFAS): This is a diagnosis that is given to those who do not meet the full criteria for FAS, but have some of the facial abnormalities and other difficulties associated with pre-natal alcohol exposure.

- Alcohol-Related Neurodevelopmental Disorder (ARND): The facial abnormalities and growth problems are not present, but development and functioning of the brain and nervous system have been affected by pre-natal alcohol exposure, resulting in difficulties including behavioural and learning problems.

- Alcohol-Related Birth Defects (ARBD): Pre-natal exposure to alcohol has resulted in problems with physical formation and development, including in the heart, kidneys, bones, hearing and vision. People with ARBD may also be diagnosed with one of the other conditions under the FASD umbrella.

FASD conditions are thought to be the most important, preventable cause of brain damage in the UK (BMA, 2016). In one study, as many as 75 per cent of children receiving medicals prior to an adoptive placement had been exposed to alcohol in the womb (Gregory *et al.*, 2015). Children with FASD conditions may struggle with attention problems, memory problems, specific language and numeracy deficits, behavioural and social challenges and sensory impairments. FASD conditions are lifelong disabilities. Children cannot be motivated out of the difficulties, or overcome them by trying harder. People whose FASD is undiagnosed or poorly understood are at risk of a range of secondary difficulties including mental health problems, poor attainment at school, alcohol and drug problems, difficulty finding and maintaining employment, higher risk of incarceration, and difficulties living independently.

When a child has experienced a traumatic, neglectful or abusive start to life, FASD conditions may be present alongside other difficulties, including attachment difficulties. It is vital that children who are at risk of FASD are screened at the earliest possible opportunity and a comprehensive package of support is put in place to enable them to achieve their potential and prevent the development of secondary difficulties. Many children with FASD do not have low IQs (Mattson and Riley, 1998) but specific difficulties prevent them from reaching their educational potential. If a child is looked-after or previously looked-after, the possibility of FASD should always be considered.

> Prior to a diagnosis of FASD and [sensory processing disorder], my son's experience at school was much less constructive and far more traumatic. Since his diagnosis he is no longer labelled as a naughty child and the school has tried extremely hard.

Pathological Demand Avoidance

Pathological Demand Avoidance (PDA) is a condition which is generally considered to be part of the autistic spectrum. A child with PDA may resist perfectly ordinary demands and requests in a variety of ways, including becoming passive, manipulating situations, becoming aggressive, becoming extremely upset, physically incapacitating themselves, procrastinating and negotiating, and withdrawing altogether. It is thought to be rooted in anxiety and an overwhelming need to remain in control. Demands made in non-negotiable ways make a child with PDA feel as though they are having the control taken away from them, which raises their anxiety levels. A child with a PDA profile may even adamantly refuse to participate in an activity they are known to enjoy.

Although PDA is not yet recognised as a discrete diagnosis, knowledge about its presentation is becoming increasingly widespread, and information about PDA can be found in many websites and publications that are focused on autism.

Speech, language and communication

Abuse, neglect and trauma have detrimental effects on a child's language development, and young children are particularly vulnerable (Sylvestre, *et al.*, 2016). As many as 28 per cent of adopted children with recognised special educational needs have speech, language and communication difficulties (Adoption UK, 2017); this is second only to social, emotional and mental health needs.

Children who have experienced complex trauma may have generalised speech and language delays, as well as specific difficulties, for instance, articulating needs and feelings, using abstract communication skills (such as sarcasm, indirect commands), processing language and understanding non-verbal cues. A child whose expressive language (how they speak and what they say) is delayed might be relatively easy to spot in a classroom, but communication difficulties also affect a child's receptive language – their ability to understand what is being said to them. Communication skills are integral to children's social, emotional and cognitive development, so speech and language difficulties can have a cumulative negative effect on other areas of development.

Language and communication is an unavoidable part of almost every aspect of school life and learning. Not only is every curriculum area full of its own terminology and vocabulary, but children will daily be required to speak, listen, read, write, record and share information, as well as navigate the plethora of non-verbal cues in a busy classroom or playground. Delays in language will clearly affect a child's progress in literacy, but can also have implications across the curriculum as they may struggle to be attentive for long periods, process language and instructions very slowly, have a limited vocabulary, lack confidence to speak out, and forget what has been said to them. Children with communication difficulties are more likely to have behaviour difficulties, more likely to struggle to maintain relationships with friends, and more likely to have low confidence and self-esteem. Behind the struggles of many frustrated, low-achieving, isolated children there may be an unrecognised speech, language or communication need.

Sensory processing difficulties

Until relatively recently, sensory processing difficulties tended to be thought of as a symptom of another condition, such as autistic spectrum disorder. However, researchers at the University of California San Francisco have identified abnormalities in the brain structure of children with sensory processing difficulties, which set it apart as an individual condition that does not arise solely as a result of other conditions (Owen *et al.*, 2013). They estimate that as many as 16 per cent of school-age children could be affected by sensory processing disorder, although this formal diagnosis is not currently available.

Without language, an infant relies on sensory input to understand the world. They receive important sensory feedback from sucking, being rocked, being touched, being swung and carried. All of this development takes place within the context of a secure attachment relationship, so it is not difficult to see that a child who experiences neglect could miss out on the building blocks of proper sensory function. For children who experience chronic trauma when they are still pre-verbal, the memories of these events are stored disjointedly as sensory fragments, meaning that later recall of the 'memories' is in the form of physical sensations and emotional reactions (van der Kolk, 2014). A young child may store sensory memories of sensations related to their traumatic experiences, which can act as triggers long after the events took place, resulting in emotional and behavioural reactions that seem to come from nowhere.

Children with sensory processing difficulties may be over- or under-sensitive to input via the five most well-known senses – touch, taste, sight, hearing, smell – and also three lesser-known internal senses: vestibular, proprioception and interoception.

The vestibular system processes information about our movement and gravity and provides feedback between the brain and the body about where we are in space, supporting our movement, balance and co-ordination.

Proprioception is a sense of body position and limb awareness. It allows us to know where our limbs are without having to look, and how much strength our muscles need to use to perform everyday tasks, maintain our posture, and correct our bodies if something unexpected happens, such as standing suddenly on an unstable surface.

Interoception relates to information that your body sends to your brain about its internal state. It helps to regulate functions such as body temperature, hunger, thirst, heart rate and digestion. Children who struggle to correctly interpret interoceptive signals may not know that they are hot, cold, hungry, thirsty or in pain. They may not recognise body signals that tell them that it is time to go to the toilet. As they are not as aware of the physical state of their bodies, it is harder for them to recognise signs of their own emotional state such as faster breathing or a thumping heart, which makes it more difficult for them to learn to regulate those emotional states. Normal feelings, such as tiredness or hunger, are misinterpreted so that a child can become distressed or even have meltdowns due to feelings of discomfort that they cannot express or find a solution to.

Children who are hyper-sensitive to sensory input may find bright lights, loud noises, scratchy clothing, and being touched, especially by surprise, intolerable. They may avoid swings and playground equipment, bump into things and seem clumsy, eat or drink too much to avoid hunger and thirst feelings, and apply too much force to simple tasks, breaking pencils and slamming things down on the desk. Overwhelming levels of sensory input can lead to meltdowns, aggressive responses and fight–flight–freeze responses.

On the other hand, children who are hypo-sensitive may engage in sensory-seeking behaviours that can easily be misinterpreted, for example, fidgeting, rocking, jumping, bumping, crashing and incessant noise-making. They may crave intense movement such as spinning or bouncing on a trampoline, or constantly touch people, objects or interesting textures, regardless of personal space. A hypo-sensitive child may not respond appropriately to pain, or not notice that their hands are freezing cold.

It is possible for a child to have a sensory difficulty in one, more or all of the senses, and for them to be hyper-sensitive in some areas while being hypo-sensitive in others. This means that the profile of children with sensory processing difficulties is enormously varied. Some children will have difficulties with sensory modulation, switching between under- and over-reaction to sensory messages because the central nervous system is not able to process them. They may also have difficulty integrating input across the senses, for instance, processing things that they can see and hear at the same time.

The school environment is often an intensely stimulating one, full of colourful displays, distracting sounds and jostling people. Children who bump into others in the lunch queue, fidget and jiggle on their seats, and whizz round and round in the playground might seem to be displaying the symptoms of Attention Deficit Hyperactivity Disorder (ADHD), but sensory processing could be at the root of their behaviour. Occupational therapy can support children to regulate their responses to sensory input by engaging them in specially designed physical activities. In school, adjustments to the environment can reduce sensory input for hyper-sensitive children to lessen the frequency with which they feel overwhelmed. Parents and carers will be able to share valuable information about their child's triggers. For hypo-sensitive children who engage in sensory-seeking behaviours, building in opportunities for sensory input regularly during the day, such as pushing or carrying something heavy, sucking, chewing or bouncing, may provide the sensory input the child is craving.

Executive functioning difficulties

When we plan, organise, make decisions, transfer from one activity to another, and control our emotional responses and impulses, we are using executive functioning. These skills rely on our working memory, our ability to sustain or shift our attention from one demand to another, our self-control and ability to resist impulsive thoughts or actions, all of which will develop through our earliest relationships and experiences. Children who have experienced neglect are more likely to have executive functioning and non-verbal reasoning difficulties lasting into adulthood (Nikulina and Widom, 2013).

Poor executive functioning means children can be disorganised, lose and forget equipment, struggle to start and complete tasks and projects, forget what they have read, process information slowly, have difficulty with transitions, lack planning skills and display poor impulse control. Many of these difficulties can mistakenly be labelled as laziness or lack of motivation. In school, children with executive functioning difficulties will need extra support to make sure they are properly equipped, scaffolding such as visual plans to help them complete tasks, modelling of desired behaviour, and extra help coping with transitions and disruptions to routine.

Physical development

Neglect and abuse in infancy and childhood can result in a range of physical delays and impairments. It is not uncommon for neglected children to be physically small in stature and delayed in meeting their milestones such as sitting, crawling and walking. Infants left lying in cribs for very long periods are unlikely to develop their core strength sufficiently, which will have a negative subsequent effect on both fine and gross motor skills. Children with poor core strength may slouch over the desk, fidget when they have to sit for long periods, struggle to climb, run and jump, have difficulties mastering handwriting, and suffer from physical fatigue. Exercises designed by an occupational therapist can develop core strength and drive improvement in a range of areas.

While neglect can cause physical developmental delays, it can also result in existing medical or developmental problems going untreated, exacerbating their effects. Missed visits to the dentist and lack of dental hygiene combined with poor diet can result in children with ongoing, painful dental problems. There may be undiagnosed visual and hearing problems which, over time, can have a significant impact on a child's ability to learn and develop in line with their peers.

Childhood neglect and abuse is also associated with problems with the immune system as stress can activate inflammatory responses in the body (Gonzalez, 2013). Adults who were abused or neglected as children face an increased risk of depression, high blood pressure, high cholesterol and coronary heart disease. The hypothalamic-pituitary-adrenocortical (HPA) axis, which handles our stress response and maintains our diurnal rhythm, responds to stress by directing energy towards survival activities, and away from less critical activities such as the immune system, growth, digestion and reproduction (Gunnar and Cheatham, 2003). For a child exposed to chronic high levels of stress, the body is spending much of its resources handling that stress, and has little left over for normal, healthy development. As the HPA axis is also vital in releasing cortisol appropriately to maintain regular sleep patterns, it is not surprising if children who have been abused and neglected struggle to sleep at night, or are excessively tired during the daytime, all of which will impact on their ability to function at school.

Special educational needs

Even from this brief overview of some of the more common diagnoses and disorders that can be caused by early complex trauma and neglect, it is clear that the needs of many affected children will not fit neatly into one special needs category. A survey of more than 2000 adoptive parents carried out by Adoption UK in 2017 found that just under half of respondents' adopted children had recognised special educational needs and disabilities (SEND), and 60 per cent of these had an Education Health and Care Plan (or equivalent). When respondents were asked to indicate all the types of special needs that applied to their child, social, emotional and mental health needs (SEMH) were by far the dominant category, applying to 63 per cent of children. However, there was then a fairly even split between other areas of need, including autistic spectrum disorders, speech, language and communication needs and specific learning difficulties, suggesting that many children had needs spreading across multiple categories.

When parents were asked to indicate only their child's primary area of need, 45 per cent selected SEMH. The national figures from the Department for Education in England suggested that in 2017, 16 per cent of children with SEND had SEMH as their primary area of need, so adopted children are significantly over-represented in this category. As the descriptions in this chapter have shown, some of the problems caused by attachment difficulties, sensory processing difficulties, FASD and other conditions can easily be interpreted as behavioural or social and emotional problems if the root cause is not known and understood. It is known that people with FASD are at risk of secondary conditions associated with poor mental health, and it is a serious concern that continuing difficulties in school may exacerbate existing mental health problems, or even create them where they did not previously exist. Adoption UK's *Bridging the Gap* report (2018) highlighted the results of a survey of more than 4000 adoptive parents and adopted children and young people. It found that 70 per cent of parents felt that their adopted child's educational progress was negatively affected by problems with their wellbeing in school, and that nearly 80 per cent of adopted children and young people agreed with the statement, 'I feel confused and worried at school.'

While existing categories of SEND may be strained when faced with children with such complex needs, the SEND Code of Practice (Department for Education, 2015) in England reminds us that 'The purpose of identification is to work out what action the school needs to take, not to fit a pupil into a category. In practice, individual children or young people often have needs that cut across all these areas and their needs may change over time' (Paragraph 6.27). Assessments of needs must be detailed, not limited by a diagnosis or lack of one, and cover the full extent of an individual's abilities and disabilities. In short, the needs of the child must be at the heart of the process.

We are lucky to have a very good school that is good at supporting children's individual needs. Our daughter has a supported play plan at lunchtimes, a care plan for her toileting and has [sensory processing therapy] each morning at the moment, as well as music therapy weekly which has been in place for two years. In addition, they manage pupil relationships and social difficulties well. Without all this, I think she would struggle at school.

BURNSIDE PRIMARY SCHOOL

Towards a school culture informed by a developing understanding of the impact of adverse childhood experiences and driven by a relentless focus on children, staff and families generating wellbeing for themselves, the environment and others

In September 2017, Burnside Primary School used Public Equity Funding to host a screening of the film, *Resilience: The Biology of Stress and the Science of Hope*,[1] which explores the link between adverse childhood experiences (ACEs) and a range of negative long-term health outcomes. The documentary also sheds light on some of the individuals, organisations and projects that are working to redress the balance for children who have been exposed to such experiences.

This screening, which was attended by 220 families as well as local councillors, coupled with extensive training for Burnside's staff team, heralded a very public declaration that Burnside was to become a trauma-informed environment for all of the children in the school. There has been a school-wide commitment to learning about the biology of behaviour and the self-regulation system, which has underpinned the introduction of strategies such as five-point regulation scales,[2] asking parents to put mobile devices away at collection times, silencing school bells, drama therapy to explore stressors and challenges, introducing key adults across each stage to promote attachment, removing 'red cards'[3] from the behaviour policy, breathing count sticks[4] for every

---

1   Released January 11 2016 in the USA, produced by KPJR Films and STK Films.
2   Five-point regulation scales are visual scales that support children to identify their emotional responses to various situations and triggers, to aid children in recognising those responses and pre-empting them with an agreed coping strategy.
3   In some behaviour management policies, children are handed 'red cards' when their behaviour does not meet the required standard. These may be displayed publicly, and may result in a sanction if an agreed number are collected.
4   Breathing count sticks are simple tools, often made with a pipe cleaner and beads, to help children regulate their breathing. Children move a bead along the length of the stick while breathing in, and then move another while breathing out.

child, worry dolls and worry boxes, extensive outdoor learning opportunities rooted in STEM (Science, Technology Engineering and Mathematics) activities, and the development of a food and clothing bank to support parents.

The school has made a commitment to developing an understanding of the synergy between learning and wellbeing. All children participated in a learners' conference which enabled the school to develop 'stuck strategies' so all children know what to do when they don't know what to do. The school also has an innovative plenary system which enables all children to set next steps in learning. Progression is shared with every family so each child has a progression narrative.

The development of the school's trauma-informed initiatives has relied heavily on partnerships both within the local community, and between the school and its families. A local Catholic church has allowed the school to use its premises for drama therapy sessions; Dr Suzanne Zeedyk [author, research scientist based at Dundee University (Scotland), and expert in attachment and child development] has facilitated training for staff, and workshops for families; Women's Aid runs weekly groups for children in the school's meeting room; NHS Tayside has delivered training for staff; local gardeners have supported the creation of a 'Burnside Berry Farm' and a 'Mandarin Garden' in the school's grounds.

However, it is in the involvement of parents, carers and the children themselves that the strength of this project may be most evident. Attendance at the workshops was supported by the provision of a crèche, widening opportunities for families to become involved in the direction the school is taking. Over 25 parents volunteer at the school on a weekly basis to support children's learning, and individual parents with expertise in the care profession have stepped forward to offer their skills. As they have become more involved in the process, head teacher, Nicky Murray, has noticed an increase in the number of parents communicating their own concerns and anxieties, and using the strategies developed within school to support them at home. Nicky describes the honesty and commitment of the school's families as both humbling and inspiring.

The children have also responded with enthusiasm, signing up to be yoga ambassadors, peer mediators, play support buddies, reading partners and 'Kitbag' experts,[5] running sessions to support other children to explore and talk about their feelings. Children's feedback is vital in monitoring the success of the various initiatives at the school. In the school's most recent inspection, 'Children's contributions as agents of change was of particular note.'

In fact, the school's latest inspection (June 2018) by Her Majesty's Inspectorate of Education (HMIe) is evidence of the progress the whole community is making. 'Leadership of change' was evaluated as sector leading, as was 'Ensuring wellbeing, quality and inclusion'. The inspector's report particularly praised the school's 'aims flower', which is focused on wellbeing indicators, and is known and used by children, staff and parents. The inspection report notes that 'This results in almost all children being calm and engaged purposefully in learning at all times' (Summarised Inspection Findings – Burnside Primary School – Angus Council).

Burnside reports through the wellbeing outcomes of safe, healthy, active, nurtured, achieving, respected, responsible and included, and has found creative ways to cultivate a language of wellbeing across the whole school community including issuing 500 school aims fridge magnets to all homes in the community with a script supporting communication in and out of school.

In the middle of the Burnside flower is the word 'GRIT' which has been used to focus the school around a common core of effort in every task and this was evident through the HMIe description of 'Highly motivated and articulate children who demonstrate an absolute commitment to be, and do their best. They are confident, responsible and show very high levels of empathy towards each other and respect for their school community. They demonstrate a high degree of resilience and readily seek out and take on new challenges.' Agency underpins every aspect of the school's work and the school is firm in supporting children and families to generate wellbeing outcomes for themselves, others and the environment.

---

5   'Kitbags' are pre-prepared bags of items to support mindfulness and resilience. In schools, children show their peers how to use the contents.

Chapter 3

RELATIONSHIPS ARE KEY

In this chapter:

The home–school relationship

Key attachment figures in school

Relationships for all

Relationships with peers

When the pressure is on to raise attainment, achieve targets and evidence progress, a focus on relationships might seem like a frivolous add-on to the serious business of education. How can we justify using precious classroom time to focus on social skills when exams are just around the corner? How can we spend funds to train all the staff in trauma-informed approaches when budgets are stretched and there isn't enough equipment to go around? Surely teachers should focus on teaching! Readers might admit to a temptation to skip over this chapter altogether, and move on in search of practical strategies to support that particular child, or manage that particular situation.

In schools, though, all strategies, interventions and learning activities take place in the context of a complex web of relationships. In fact, all of life takes place within the context of relationships. Those relationships are important to us, not just because they are nice things to have, but because the success or otherwise of them is a huge contributor to our wellbeing, self-esteem, feelings of contentment, security, and ability to take risks and try new things with confidence.

Paying attention to promoting positive and nurturing relationships in school does not detract from academic achievement; it actually supports and encourages it. Regardless of their background, children with higher levels of emotional and social wellbeing achieve better academically, and are more engaged in school. Conversely, children who are bullied or do not have positive friendships with their peers are less engaged at school (Gutman and Vorhaus, 2012). If we are to help children from very difficult backgrounds to aim high and achieve, then we need to recognise that their path to that achievement may begin with the quality of relationships they are provided with in schools. Progress and attainment in learning are rewards in themselves, leading to increased levels of self-esteem and confidence in children and creating an upward ladder of success. For many struggling children, the route to getting a foot on the first rung of that ladder will lie in relationships.

Two studies carried out in the US provide an insight into the effect of teacher–student relationships on the academic progress of primary-aged students. Fryer (2018) tracked the attainment and progress of children in schools where teachers specialised in particular subjects, seeing several classes each day, rather like the secondary school model. This system was called 'platooning' in the study. Twenty-three elementary schools adopted platooning for two years, and the outcomes of students were compared with schools with nearly identical prior standardised test results where the same teachers stayed with their class all day in the traditional way. Although it may have been assumed that using highly specialised teachers would increase students' attainment, in fact both the reading and maths skills of the children who had been taught by specialists were lower after two years than their peers using the traditional method. Platooning schools also saw an increase in absences and exclusions, and children with special educational needs were disproportionately negatively affected.

In conclusion, Fryer noted that teacher specialisation in primary schools 'decreases student achievement, decreases student attendance, and increases student behavioural problems'. Some teachers using the platooning model said that they considered themselves less able to provide students with individual attention, and reported a reduction in job satisfaction, raising the possibility that the benefits brought by the increased expertise of the teachers were negatively outweighed by the difficulties platooning created in terms of forming relationships with the students, and knowing them well enough to provide individualised, tailored support.

Elsewhere in the US, a study following groups of children who retained the same elementary school teacher for two years (Hill and Jones, 2018) found that this practice led to a small but significant increase in test scores. This effect was particularly noticeable for vulnerable students, and even children who entered the class partway through the two years benefited from the effects, suggesting that retaining the class teacher resulted in an improved general learning environment. These are just two studies, but they add to the wealth of data we already have that demonstrates that attending to children's social and emotional wellbeing in the context of relationships is a prerequisite for engagement and subsequently improving attainment.

Think about your own school days. No matter how long ago they were, you will probably have some vivid memories of certain teachers. The schools I attended seemed to be populated by a particularly colourful cast of characters: the fierce but enthralling Year 6 teacher who called all the girls 'petal' and 'flower', wore impossibly high stilettos, and led the hymn singing in assemblies with an operatic voice; the Science teacher with a penchant for hand-knitted jumpers in surprising and sometimes barely appropriate designs; the Religious Education (RE) teacher who delivered lessons in a numbing monotone, all the while breathing out the fumes of the menthol lozenges we assumed he was using to hide the smell of a lunchtime snifter.

We had some kind of relationship with each one of those teachers. We formed opinions and ideas about them, and developed ways of relating to them, just as they did towards us. Some of our teachers made us feel miserable and, with hindsight, I'm sure we made some of them feel miserable too. Some of them we manipulated shamelessly. One of our secondary school teachers could easily be provoked to shouting rages. It was the weekly mission of some of the students to wind him up to a red-faced explosion and then sit back and snigger at the results, while others cringed and cowered, traumatised by the display.

During difficult times, though, teachers and other members of school staff can become safe havens for children. It might be the kindly face and genuine greeting of a member of the office staff as a child signs in late again because their caring duties have overwhelmed their morning, or the pastoral mentor who checks in with a struggling student throughout the day, or the school librarian who finds extra jobs at lunchtime for the child who is being bullied in the playground.

For children who have experienced relational trauma caused by abuse, neglect, insecure attachments and loss, relationships are key. As Betsy de Thierry (2017, p.27) succinctly puts it, 'When a person has been hurt in a relationship, they can only be healed in a relationship.' It is especially sad, then, that children who have experienced trauma within their most important relationships often go on to find it extremely difficult to form and maintain supportive, nurturing relationships with others. The very thing they need to heal, grow and develop is the very thing that is almost impossibly hard for them to achieve. If such children are to survive and thrive in school, the quality of the network of relationships around them will be of paramount importance.

The home–school relationship

A fluid, responsive and mutually respectful home–school relationship is the bedrock on which a traumatised child's school experience will be built. A child's parents or carers, and their educators, each have their own expertise, and bringing these together is vital. 'Successful partnerships acknowledge that everyone's expertise is welcomed and necessary with each party bringing their own perspective to the table' (Gore Langton and Boy, 2017, p.129).

Parents and carers know their child best. Some parents and carers are also extremely well-versed in the impact of trauma and neglect on children's development. Training for foster carers and adoptive parents includes elements of this, and it is not uncommon for carers and adoptive parents to read widely on the subject. From a teacher's perspective, it may feel overwhelming to be given leaflets and books to study by a concerned parent which only seem to add to an already crowded workload, but it is likely the parent will already have studied that material, synthesised it, and have a good idea of how it specifically relates to their child. Where the expertise of both parties is respected, the parent can be encouraged to summarise and present the information to key staff members, and then the educators can bring their expertise to bear in relating that information to the school environment.

Our child has made an excellent start to school and is academically ahead of most of her peers. However, we work in education and have really supported her learning. We are well aware that her emotional wellbeing is most challenging for her as she understands more of her story, and we try to inform school with literature and information on therapeutic approaches and the impact of trauma. They are keen to be an adoption-friendly school and we hope to work with them. Our child has experienced major trauma and loss and we think her mental health issues will arise as she goes through school so we want to equip school with as much information as possible.

Some parents and carers have access to outside expertise which may not be available in school. There may be social workers or other professionals assigned to the family, involvement with child and adolescent mental health services (CAMHS) or other therapeutic providers and, in the case of previously looked-after children, support services funded by the Adoption Support Fund (in England). Schools can gain valuable insights from these specialised services which can be added to information gathered from school-based assessment and support services.

Communications between home and school need to be both strategic and procedural. Strategic communications support planning and whole-school approaches, and can be facilitated by regular meetings between parents or carers and key members of school staff. This type of communication should start, if possible, before the child begins at the school, and continue throughout their time there, even if everything seems to be running smoothly. Systems such as Personal Education Plans (an ongoing record of how professionals around a child will support their education) can support this strategic communication for looked-after children, and similar systems could be considered for previously looked-after children and others in clear need, whether they have recognised SEND or not. Initial meetings when the child starts school ensure that all relevant information is known and shared, where appropriate, and subsequent routine meetings will establish and develop relationships between school and home so that if difficulties arise, the support network is already in place. These meetings can be used to plan for known events such as transitions at the end of year or school, monitor the effectiveness of existing strategies, develop new strategies to accommodate changing situations, and discuss how support and funding, such as Pupil Premium Plus (additional funding given to schools in England to support looked-after and previously looked-after children), can best be used.

Procedural communications are more short-term, and can support both parents and schools to manage day-to-day situations and share current information. When parents are well-informed about what is happening in school – theme days, substitute teachers, class visitors, changes to routine – they can prepare their child and support them to manage the disruption to their routine. Children who have experienced trauma may have difficulty recalling and recounting the events of the day, so regular communications from school about what the child did that day can foster positive conversations about school at home.

These frequent (perhaps daily) procedural communications need to be carried out sensitively. No parent wants to experience the 'walk of shame' across the playground in response to a beckoning teacher. Parents and carers of children with difficulties can sometimes feel judged and ashamed in front of other parents, tone of voice can be misinterpreted in written communications if relationships are tense, and letters sent home can sometimes be lost before the child leaves the building if executive functioning skills are lacking.

When the context of communications is that of a supportive, mutually respectful relationship between school and home, misinterpretations and tensions are less likely to arise. Schools can support this by sharing the positive as well as the problems so that parents and carers do not learn to dread the school's number flashing up on their mobile phones. An agreed format for regular communication can prevent both the teacher and the parent from becoming overwhelmed. For instance, the class teacher might agree to phone the parent once a week to give an update, a daily home–school book could be maintained, or it could be agreed that email communications will all be funnelled through a specific member of staff. It can also be useful to agree in advance on what type of information will be shared.

Responsive home–school communication can be a powerful defence against triangulation, where a child attempts to play one adult off against another by, perhaps, telling different versions of the same story to different adults, or going along with an adult's misinterpretation of events in order to elicit sympathy or avoid punishment. This can be as simple as a child claiming their parent did not wash their uniform when in fact they just didn't want to conform to that rule on that day but, taken to extremes, can have serious consequences for parents and carers as well as for school staff if allegations are made.

In all communications between schools and families, maintaining a non-judgemental attitude is vital. As Gore Langton and Boy (2017, p.134) put it, 'we can sometimes reach a gridlock where the school believes that the problem is the parents and the parents believe that the problem is the school. The first step to getting unstuck again is agreeing that the problem is the *problem*.' Trauma is a tricky customer. It can make the impact of historical events appear to be caused by current events, can hide itself in one place but unleash itself with force in another, and drive those living and working with children affected by it into new trauma of their own. Many parents and carers of traumatised children are parenting through significant challenges, and trauma-informed schools can play a crucial and unique role in supporting the whole family.

Key attachment figures in school

While any child's primary attachment relationship ought to be with their main caregivers, children will form some level of attachment in their other relationships as well, including with teachers and staff at the schools where they spend hours each day. Far from being discouraged, these secondary attachment relationships are vital if traumatised children are to experience school as a 'safe base' from which they can explore, learn and grow.

Children who have experienced early trauma may arrive at school unprepared to trust adults, feeling unsafe, and highly anxious. In the case of younger looked-after, adopted and previously looked-after children, their attachment relationships with their carers or parents may only be at a fledgling stage of development, and then they are separated from them for hours each week at school. Children with attachment difficulties of any age will benefit from additional support from an 'attachment figure' or 'key adult' in school, to act as a safe base and be available for them.

Much is said about children being 'school ready', or becoming independent, but before independence must come healthy dependence. Children who have not experienced a healthy dependent relationship in their infancy and early childhood do not have the building blocks in place to develop healthy independence. Bombèr (2007, p.59) emphasises the need for schools to allow 'dependency in school appropriate to the child's emotional rather than chronological age'. The key adult in school provides a quality relationship that can build on and support the development of attachments with parents and carers, but not replace it.

The key adult should be somebody who is available to have regular interactions with the child. It could be a teaching assistant, learning mentor, pastoral support worker, or even a non-teaching member of staff. It should not be a member of staff who has a wide responsibility for many children, such as the class teacher or Special Educational Needs Co-ordinator (SENCO), as this can create conflict when the teacher is engaged with other children, and can also have the danger of making the child in question appear to be the 'teacher's pet' in the classroom. Allowing the child some say in the choice of adult may be appropriate, especially if the child is of secondary school age. There is no benefit in forcing a relationship where either party is not engaged in the process.

Whoever fulfils the role, consistency is key. Regularly changing teaching assistant assignments and rotating 1–1 support staff in an attempt to stop pupils becoming too dependent is counter-productive for children who have experienced trauma. Change is threatening and frightening if a child has insecure foundations, and real independence (rather than the learned self-sufficiency of the traumatised child) must follow healthy dependence. It will, of course, be necessary at some point for the child to become more independent but their route to that, and the time frames involved, may be significantly different from that of other children. Staff absence and turnover is unavoidable, however, and the availability of a secondary person, who the child knows and has a relationship with, can be helpful when the key adult cannot be available.

The role and importance of the key adult is a significant and complex one, and both Bombèr (2007) and Gore Langton and Boy (2017) provide detailed overviews of the expectations, activities and challenges involved in successfully supporting an individual child in this way. The role is not that of a therapist or counsellor, and neither does it replace the work of the teacher, but it may involve 'checking in' with a child to show them that they are held in mind throughout the day, using strategies to de-escalate potential flashpoints and conflicts or to manage the fallout after they have happened, reinforcing stability and routine, and supporting communications between all the adults involved in a child's education, including parents and carers. They are to be a safe base for the child in the school environment.

It is essential that the role of the key adult is recognised and supported throughout the school, from the top down. They must be predictably available for the child they are supporting, which means that time given to this should not be compromised by other activities or duties, and they should be included in meetings about and planning for the child. All relationships carry with them an emotional cost, as well as a cost of time and effort, and the key adult relationship is no exception. Children who have experienced trauma and insecure attachment can have intense feelings which can, in turn, provoke similar intensity of emotion in those who are living and working with them. It is vital that key adults are effectively trained for the role, well-supported within the school and given opportunity to talk about the challenges they face without judgement.

Relationships for all

Discussion of the key adult role should not be taken to imply that other members of staff have no part to play. Of course, it would not be appropriate, practical or helpful for all adults in a school to attempt to form close relationships with every child, but the participation of all staff members will be necessary if the environment of the school is to be attuned and responsive to the needs of all children, and especially those who have experienced trauma and insecure attachments.

> The school has been excellent from the moment my eldest son arrived, with regular meetings between the head, class teacher, pastoral care manager and ourselves to ensure all of his needs were being met. Unfortunately, my second son was diagnosed with cancer in November, and the school immediately implemented extra emotional support for my oldest every single day with one-to-one pastoral time timetabled into his day; they knew and adapted for his difficulty in discussing emotions.

Beyond the teaching and classroom staff, there are a plethora of other adults who children interact with on a daily basis, from the office staff to the lunchtime supervisors. When training on trauma and attachment is being considered, it is essential that all adult members of the school community are included, not just teachers, or members of staff with special responsibilities. Unstructured time can be a particular flashpoint, with 60 per cent of adoptive parents reporting that their child has difficulties during breaks and lunchtimes (Adoption UK, 2018), so involvement of playground and lunchtime supervisors is essential. If trauma-informed approaches are embedded across the whole school, informing every relationship and interaction with every child, then it will not be necessary to share confidential information on the backgrounds of individual children with every adult in the school.

Although most teachers in a school will not fulfil the role of key adult to individual children, every teacher has a responsibility to know and understand the children in their classrooms so that they are best placed to provide the optimum conditions for the children to learn and make progress. As we have seen in previous chapters, the challenges facing many children who have experienced trauma in early childhood go far beyond attachment alone. An attachment-aware approach in the classroom and across the school will do much to benefit children who have experienced trauma and insecure attachments, but the knowledge and expertise of the teachers will also need to be utilised to identify and support children who may be experiencing challenges caused by Foetal Alcohol Spectrum Disorder (FASD), sensory processing difficulties, executive functioning difficulties and other implications of adverse childhood experiences that are not wholly rooted in attachment. While a child with FASD may benefit from an attachment-aware approach and provision of a key adult, those strategies will not cure their disability. Above all, teachers, all teachers, must really know the children in front of them so that, in an attuned and sensitive relationship, they can go on to identify and address additional difficulties and challenges that the child might be presenting with. Admittedly, this can be more difficult in a secondary setting with children shuttling between classrooms several times per day, and the role of the SENCO, designated teacher or key adult will be even more vital in ensuring that all teachers who have contact with children with additional needs have all the information and strategies at their disposal.

Relationships with peers

The ever-shifting world of peer relationships will present challenges to most children at some point in their school life. Children who have not had the experience of supportive and nurturing relationships in their early childhood do not have a model for how such relationships should function. This impacts not only their relationships with adults, but also with their peers. In addition, developmental and social and emotional delay can make starting and maintaining positive friendships with children their own age extremely difficult.

Some children will, therefore, arrive at school without the skills needed to participate in play, banter, sharing and turn-taking. They may behave and respond in ways that the other children do not understand, and misinterpret other children's actions and behaviours. They may be developmentally much younger than their chronological age and do much better relating to children younger than themselves. Just like the skills of reading and writing, these social skills will not develop by magic, but will require the intervention and support of the adults in the school.

Unstructured time can be very unsettling for children who need routine, structure and boundaries in order to feel safe and contained. Primary-aged children may benefit from being actively shown how to play, as one would a much younger child. Zoning playgrounds and providing plenty of hands-on adult support and structured activities can support children into a positive experience of play and peer relationships which can be built on to develop more independent play later. As with the key adult role, the aim is to put in the missing foundations now so that children can manage independently in future.

Even at secondary school, support during unstructured times may be necessary. This could take the form of giving children jobs that enable them to feel valued, involving them in clubs and extra-curricular activities, or providing a 'safe space' where children can go to socialise, talk and cool off if necessary.

Bullying can be a serious problem for children who are different in any way. Two-thirds of secondary-aged adopted children have reported that they have been teased or bullied at school because of their adopted status, and parents have reported that adopted children have attempted suicide as a result of bullying (Adoption UK, 2018). Teasing, name calling and bullying a child for being looked-after, adopted or cared for outside of the birth home should be viewed as seriously as any other targeted bullying in schools. Opportunities can be taken within the school curriculum to educate all children about what it means to be looked-after or adopted, and to emphasise that teasing or bullying on these grounds is unacceptable in the school.

CHEADLE PRIMARY SCHOOL

Towards a relationship-focused school culture

Karen Leech, head teacher at 300-pupil Cheadle Primary School, believes strongly that each child is an individual and should be catered for according to their individual needs. Forming relationships with children and their families is crucial to the school's approach. Karen is clear that children at Cheadle Primary School receive bespoke provision and are treated according to their needs, and this philosophy extends to all the children, not only those who are particularly vulnerable. Although there are strategies and support systems embedded in the school that are available to all, Karen stresses that Cheadle 'is not a one-size-fits-all school,' and that the success of their approach is based on 'lots of little things, depending on the needs of the child'.

All children benefit from a long-running transition support programme to help them make the move from one class to the next in the new school year. All classes will move to their new classroom and teacher a week before the end of the summer term, following a month of visits and activities designed to help them get used to their new learning environment. Parents are particularly supportive of this model, which works well for all children, but particularly for emotionally vulnerable children who may otherwise spend their entire summer holidays in a state of anxiety about returning to school in September.

The school has invested in staff training, both in attachment and trauma-awareness, and also in specific strategies to support struggling students. There are staff members trained in counselling, and in sandplay therapy on the premises, and these services are made available to any child experiencing difficulties, whether those difficulties stem from early trauma, or a current crisis. At playtimes, additional members of staff use bespoke interventions to support children who are struggling. For instance, children may be supported to spend part of the lunchtime on the playground and then be invited to join in an organised and supervised activity driven by their own interests for the rest of the time, ensuring that they avoid conflict in the playground and return to class calm and ready to learn.

Cheadle is already a UNICEF Children's Rights Respecting school, but they are always looking to improve their practice, and have recently embarked on the Attachment and Trauma Sensitive Schools Award Bronze programme. Karen is also keen to utilise the expertise of her staff. After observing a colleague's innovative and very successful lesson based on the book, *Have You Filled a Bucket Today?* (McCloud and Messing, 2015), she is now looking to roll out similar lessons designed to support mental health and wellbeing across the school.

In fact, recognising the efforts of her staff, and promoting their wellbeing and work–life balance is foundational to the school's efforts to support vulnerable children. 'Teaching is a demanding job and can be emotionally draining. We have to recognise that staff also need to be in the right mental and emotional place to teach, just as the children need to be in the right mental and emotional place to learn,' says Karen. The school has a culture of looking after staff wellbeing, seeking less time-consuming ways to complete bureaucratic tasks, and supporting staff to manage their work–life balance, within the constraints of a busy school schedule. For instance, staff members are given opportunities to complete work at home when they are not timetabled, and a recently introduced computerised system for data and administration means that certain tasks can now be completed at a time and place that works for the individual staff member, rather than, as previously, at staff meetings. The staff team at Cheadle is very stable, with a very low turnover, which Karen puts down to the supportive culture within the school, and the emphasis on developing relationships not just with children and families, but within the staff team as well.

Karen is very clear about the message she gives to parents who are considering Cheadle for their children. 'Firstly, we make sure that we keep our children safe; then we look after their mental health and wellbeing needs and then we consider learning. If the first two are not securely in place, children are not in a position to learn well.' As an adoptive parent herself, Karen is open about her own situation, and the struggles her child has faced in education. The school has a number of adopted children which Karen believes could be due in part to the reputation that they are developing locally as a school that provides excellent outcomes for struggling children. 'When I tell carers and adoptive parents that I'm an adopter too, I often see a look of relief spread across their faces. They know that their child's needs are going to be understood here, and that we recognise the particular challenges that they are facing as a family.'

Chapter 4

THINKING DIFFERENTLY

In this chapter:

PACE

Non-Violent Resistance

Windows of tolerance

Regulate, Relate, Reason

Recognising that there may be underlying reasons for unacceptable behaviour is not the same as declaring that behaviour acceptable. Parents and carers who are raising children with a history of abuse, neglect, disrupted attachments and trauma face the challenge of both understanding the causes and roots of their children's difficulties while also supporting them to learn different ways of responding and reacting. While adverse experiences in early childhood can cause children to develop maladaptive ways of viewing themselves and the world, the brain remains plastic, and it is possible to over-write pathways learned in adversity with new ways of thinking and reacting. However, this does not happen by magic, and it does not happen overnight. It takes years of patient un-learning and re-learning in a process sometimes called therapeutic re-parenting.

In this chapter, we will explore some alternative ways of parenting hurt and traumatised children that may provide insights that are also useful in a classroom setting. However, we do so with the caveat that, although these approaches can do much to support children with developmental trauma and attachment difficulties towards a better internal working model of themselves and their worlds, they do not undo neurological damage caused, for instance, by pre-natal alcohol exposure, and they are not foolproof strategies that will work on any child at any time. The four approaches outlined here represent ways of thinking about children's behaviour in the context of their past experiences, and provide a basis for moving towards changes in behaviour in ways that are founded in understanding the root causes and addressing them.

PACE

Developed by Dr Daniel Hughes, PACE parenting is an approach that prioritises relationships and a child's feeling of safety and security in order to explore their strong feelings and challenging behaviours and move towards managing these more effectively and expressing them in healthier ways. The mnemonic stands for Playfulness, Acceptance, Curiosity and Empathy. It is an approach that focuses on the child, rather than the behaviour, and builds in self-reflection skills necessary to separating out behavioural actions from thoughts and feelings, and choosing different actions in future. Throughout the process, the child is supported to feel safe and secure by an adult alongside them.

Playfulness in this context goes beyond simply playing with children or having a jokey attitude. It refers to a tone of voice, a light-hearted approach to interactions and challenging situations, and expressing joy and delight in one another. It might help to think about the playful interactions a parent might have with a baby or toddler. Approaching children with playfulness opens the possibility of joy and fun in lives that might previously have been singularly joyless, and can be a powerful tool in defusing situations that are threatening to become explosive. Playfulness can be very difficult to achieve in the face of a child's persistent challenging behaviour, and its lack can lead to relationships between adults and children that are characterised by nagging, irritability, escalation of minor difficulties, and a general lack of joy or pleasure in each other's company.

The second element, unconditional acceptance, demonstrates to the child that they are safe and that their thoughts and feelings are accepted by the adult, even if their actions are not. It works on the premise that feelings are not good or bad, right or wrong; they simply 'are'. It is possible to set very firm limits around behaviour, while neutrally accepting the feelings and thoughts that might have led to that behaviour.

Curiosity is the process by which the adult supports the child to understand the 'why' of their behaviour. Asking children directly why they did certain things can often be unproductive. They may not know why they acted as they did, and questions about their motives put them under pressure, which can result in them making up a reason, or feeling cornered and going further into behaviour driven by anxiety or rage. Curiosity allows adults to become behaviour detectives alongside the child, travelling together on a path towards understanding. It must be done calmly and without judgement. The aim is to support the child to accept that their behaviour does not mean that they are 'bad', but that it is a reaction to a thought or feeling and could perhaps be communicated in a different way.

Finally, empathy allows a child to feel an adult's compassion for their state. The child may be experiencing difficult thoughts, or strong negative feelings, but the adult acknowledges these and remains emotionally present for the child despite this.

Each of these elements does not have to be present in every single interaction with a child. Rather they can be seen as underpinning characteristics of a relationship that raises a child's sense of safety and security, and provides the best platform for re-framing behavioural challenges over time.

Approaches to try

- Playfulness, as long as it is not perceived as teasing, can defuse tense situations very effectively. For instance, if a child slams their book down on the desk, try making eye contact, smiling and then saying (without sarcasm) something like, 'Once more – with feeling this time!' Playfulness like this restores connection in a way that reprimanding a child cannot, but still makes the point. However, it takes a good judge of a situation to be sure that a child will respond in kind, and not view the comment as a challenge!

- If a child is visibly upset or hurt, acknowledge their feelings, rather than rushing too quickly to tell them that they are, or will be, fine. Accept where they are in the moment, and name their feelings if possible. For example, 'I see you have had an argument with your friend and what they said has hurt you and made you feel angry.' This is more meaningful than brushing off a child's feelings, and opens the way to exploring their emotions and reactions.

- Be curious about children and their interests and lives, not just in times of crisis, but as a way of developing relationship and increasing connection.

- Try 'I wonder...' phrases. For example, 'I see you have pushed your work across the table. You seem angry and frustrated right now [acceptance, empathy]. I wonder if you are worried that the work is too hard for you [curiosity].'

Non-Violent Resistance

Famously used by Mahatma Gandi and Martin Luther King, Non-Violent Resistance (NVR) as a philosophy aims to resolve difficult or conflict-laden situations without resorting to further aggression or violence. In a family context, it is adapted as an approach to parenting that has been found especially helpful for families experiencing anger, controlling behaviour, violence and aggression from children and young people. The approach prioritises the relationship between the parent and the child, focusing on increasing and maintaining 'parental presence' both physically, and in the mind of the child, while at the same time anchoring the whole family within an extended supportive network that may include wider family, friends, community, churches, schools and professionals. The NVR approach can be especially effective where the 'balance of power' in the relationship between an adult and a child has shifted so that the child seems to be always in control, and the adult is reduced to mainly responding to an agenda set by the child, feeling powerless and helpless.

The entire programme as it applies to families may be difficult to reproduce wholesale in the classroom. However, there are elements of it that might be usefully adapted:

- The announcement – This is a formal statement from the adult to the child about a particular priority behaviour. The statement or conversation should open with positives (for example, things that the child is doing well), before moving on to a description of the specific target behaviour and what needs to be changed, accompanied by a commitment from the adult to support the child in making the changes. It should end with a positive reflection on how things might improve for the child (and everybody else) if the changes are made and sustained.

- De-escalation skills – These begin with the adult developing skills to manage their own emotional responses to conflict situations, and then employing strategies to keep everyone safe and, if possible defuse situations, such as through using humour, playfulness or distraction. The aim here is to keep everyone calm, and avoid allowing situations to escalate to an explosive point.

- Deferred response – This is choosing to postpone dealing with the issue until later, when emotions are calmer, and responses can be planned, well considered, and delivered more dispassionately.

- Support network – In families, NVR approaches depend on the parents or carers building a strong support network of people who are kept fully aware of the difficulties faced by the family. Members of this network may be invited to sensitively speak to the child about unacceptable behaviours and support the parent or carer in their actions. This reinforces to the child that unacceptable behaviour is unacceptable everywhere, and to everybody. In school, support networks could include members of the senior leadership team, pastoral team, special educational needs team, key adults, and the family of the child, for instance.

- Prioritising target behaviours – Sometimes children will present with a whole range of behaviours that are difficult to deal with in the classroom. Some of these will cause significant disruption, while others may be technically a breach of the school rules, while not being overly disruptive. It is overwhelming for both the child and the adults involved to attempt to manage and correct every single one of these challenges at the same time. The NVR approach is to prioritise one or two 'red flag' behaviours and focus entirely on those, on the basis that it is better to effectively overcome one serious behaviour than it is to try but fail to manage every single difficulty. Priority behaviours would be the subject of an announcement (see above). Strategies are put in place, and the situation is regularly reviewed. Once the specified target behaviour seems to be under control, move on to another on the list. NVR suggests three categories for behaviours. Priority behaviours (one or two at most) take the main focus. Middle-range behaviours (around five) are more negotiable, depending on the circumstances, but will usually not be ignored. The lowest priority behaviours are ignored for now. As priority behaviours are brought under control, other behaviours can be moved up the priority list.

The NVR approach is gaining popularity among adoptive parents, kinship carers and foster carers, and some local authorities and post-adoption support services are now offering comprehensive training courses for parents, carers and professionals. If the parents or carers of a child in school are using NVR at home, it is likely that the school will form part of the supportive network, so being familiar with at least the basics of the approach will be desirable.

Windows of tolerance

The term 'window of tolerance', coined by Dr Daniel Siegel (2012, p.253), is a framework within which we can understand body and brain reactions to stress, anxiety and adversity. At its simplest, an individual's window of tolerance is the emotional state within which they can experience and manage the normal ups and downs of life, including stresses, pain, exhaustion, sadness and anger. Most of the time, we remain within our window. Difficult times may bring us to the edges of the window, but our own regulation systems and strategies will serve to bring us back to equilibrium.

If we experience extreme stressors, we can move out of our windows of tolerance, and find it very difficult to get back into equilibrium. This can result in hyper-arousal (anxiety, panic, restlessness, sleeplessness) or hypo-arousal (shutting down, lethargy, exhaustion, depression). Once we are stuck outside of our windows of tolerance, we can flip forwards and backwards between hyper and hypo-arousal, perhaps becoming driven to seek external solutions to our dysregulated state.

For children who have experienced trauma and adverse childhood experiences, the window of tolerance may be narrower than it is for those who have experienced security and stability. Children may go outside of their window with less provocation, and remain outside it for longer, stuck there without the ability to regulate themselves back into equilibrium. These children need adult help both to move back within their window and, over time, to increase the width of it so that they can stay within it more often.

When considering children's challenging behaviour in the classroom, an understanding of the window of tolerance metaphor is useful in helping us to avoid escalation of situations, and to consider the most effective responses to the behaviour. Fear, anxiety, change, transitions, sensory overload and a whole host of other triggers can catapult a child out of their window. Once that happens, attempting to reason with a child, appealing to logic or imposing consequences rooted in cause-and-effect thinking, is likely to have limited results. The child needs to come back into their window before the problem can be dealt with.

Approaches to try

- Deep and slow breathing, using the diaphragm (place hands on the tummy and watch them move).

- Sucking, chewing and crunching (drinking a smoothie or yoghurt through a straw, crunching raw carrots).

- Bouncing or rhythmic activity (jumping on a mini trampoline, star jumps, drumming, marching, rocking chair, dancing).

- Listening to calming music or rhythmic poetry.

- Sensory play, such as with water or sand.

- Heavy pushing, carrying and pulling activities.

Regulate, Relate, Reason

Coined by Dr Bruce Perry (2017), the three Rs of 'Regulate, Relate, Reason' act as a handy reminder to support interventions when children are behaving unacceptably as a result of overwhelm, fear, anxiety, or having gone outside of their window of tolerance for any reason. When we are faced with children exhibiting challenging and disruptive behaviour, it is tempting to jump straight to logic, explaining why their behaviour is inappropriate, making demands, laying out consequences, attempting to motivate children to change their ways.

However, if a child is in a state of hyper- or hypo-arousal, moving into a fight–flight–freeze response, then their brains and their bodies jump to basic survival mode, reacting instinctively, driven by adrenaline. In that state, reasoning with them is futile. The first step is to help them to regulate; bring them back into their window of tolerance, perhaps using some of the strategies outlined above, coupled with reassuring words, genuine listening and an empathic approach.

Once the child begins to regulate, then it is time to reinforce relationships. A child is much more likely to listen to your reason if they are calm, and if they feel a sense of connection to you. The relationship between a student and a teacher is obviously not the same as that between a child and a parent, but it does exist. It might be rooted in mutual respect, genuine shared interest, shared goals around achievement, learning or extra-curricular activities. The 'relate' stage is an opportunity to re-establish the mutual, respectful relationship between adult and child or young person, and can take place over a shared activity, such as clearing up in the classroom, tidying the stationery cupboard, or simply a walk and talk. The aim is to re-focus joint energies on fighting the problem, not each other.

Finally, the child is ready to hear your reason. This is the point at which problem solving can take place, plans for avoiding this situation in future can be agreed, and consequences can be discussed with less risk of escalating the situation once more.

As we move now into explorations of specific situations that might arise in a school setting, the principles outlined in this chapter should be held in mind. Taking an attachment- and trauma-aware approach to your classroom does not, and should not, mean allowing challenging behaviour to go on unchecked, but re-framing the way we think about traumatised children's behavioural patterns can lead us to strategies that will ultimately be more effective in creating the calm, orderly, learning-focused classrooms that we all need and want.

Chapter 5

SETTLING IN

In this chapter:

Setting up your room

Gathering information

Building relationships

Expectations

Effective interventions and support from the start

Both teachers and students instinctively know that the first few weeks in a new class or school are fundamental to building the relationships and the understanding that will underpin the rest of the school year. As a teacher, you have to set the tone for your classroom, while faced with rows of children about whom you may know relatively little. The pressure to get off on the right foot is intense. This same pressure can be intense for many children too, especially if they are carrying the baggage from a difficult previous year, or from a bad time at their last school.

Each new school year is a chance for a fresh start for everybody. It's a good opportunity for bad habits to be abandoned, poor reputations to be forgotten, and a new and more positive path to be carved out. Unfortunately, all of this is taking place in the midst of a great transition, and transitions, as we shall see in Chapter 7, can bring additional stress and anxiety for children who have hidden disabilities or attachment difficulties, or who have experienced loss, abuse, neglect and trauma. For this reason, it is even more vital to carefully manage the settling-in period to a new class or a new school for these most vulnerable children.

Setting up your room

The way you set up your classroom will depend on a number of factors, including the age of the children you are teaching, any particular equipment relevant to your subject, and your own preferences and teaching style. However, a few alterations with traumatised children in mind can make your classroom environment one that lessens anxiety and stress, and promotes safety, inclusion and learning:

- Incorporate a calm-zone or chillout area in the classroom. This works particularly well in zoned primary classrooms, and could incorporate a bean bag, some books, some sensory toys, a small play tent or some music to listen to with headphones.

- Hyper-vigilant and anxious children often benefit from sitting in locations where they can quickly scan the classroom, including the door, and will not have people moving behind them. Ensure that you have some seating available near the back of the room and near a wall, without a walkway or activity area behind it. If you do not have your own classroom, but move around the school, consider how seating plans for each class might be arranged to benefit hyper-vigilant children.

- Classrooms can be visually stimulating places for children with sensory processing difficulties. Consider limiting the number and busyness of displays, and create an area of low visual stimulation within the classroom.

- Having said that, do make space on your displays for a visual class timetable; add photos of the children doing the timetabled activities when available.

- Show the classroom code of conduct on the wall, with pictorial or written (as appropriate) examples of children doing 'the right thing' which can be added to as the year goes on.

- Have a large clock positioned where every child can easily see it, which you can use as a visual reference point to help children manage their time and predict the end point of activities and tasks.

- Label cupboards, drawers and other storage areas with picture clues and words so that all children can find what they need quickly and easily.

- Plan routines for daily activities, and have a visual display showing each stage.

- Make sure that things the children will need to access regularly, such as the rubbish bin, the hand-in tray or box, and any stationery equipment are easily accessible, and not likely to create a bottleneck when children are moving around.

- Check the layout of your room to make sure that you haven't created a potential 'running track' or unnecessary open spaces where children might congregate and cause a distraction.

- Some children will need frequent interactions with their teacher, perhaps because they find it difficult to focus, lose track of where they are in their work, or because of attachment-seeking behaviours. Plan seating so that you have easy access to those children's working areas.

- If your teaching time regularly involves children sitting on the floor, such as for circle time, ensure that there are spaces where children with poor core strength, or sensory processing difficulties, can be properly supported into a good seated posture.

- Consider where you will stand or sit when carrying out different tasks, such as introducing whole-class activities, writing on the board, or working with groups. Can you easily see around the classroom from all positions?

- Make sure everything is in place to begin your routines from the first day. This could include coat pegs, labelled storage areas, drawers or trays for work to be handed in and class rotas.

- If you plan to change any aspect of your room after the new school year has started, make sure all children are informed about the changes in advance.

Gathering information

Unless the children in your classes are transferring from another school, the chances are you will already know a fair bit about some of them by reputation, or from comments your colleagues may have made in the staffroom, or because of your own observations around the school corridors and open areas. Now is the time to put all of these pre-conceived ideas to one side. All children respond in a variety of ways to different situations and to different adults. The experiences that your colleague has had with a particular child are not necessarily going to match your experiences with the same child. The shocking behaviour you witnessed from a particular child in the dinner queue that one time may have been the result of a never-to-be-repeated confluence of circumstances. Children with a well-established reputation need the chance for a fresh start as they begin a new school year, so when you begin gathering necessary information about the children who will be coming into your class, try to do so with an open mind. This might be the year that everything changes for that child who has so far struggled throughout their school career.

Most of the children in any classroom will have experienced adults as being mainly safe, reliable and consistent, and will be ready to relate to you, as the teacher, on that basis. They are likely to settle into the new class and new routines fairly quickly, adapt easily to your expectations, and soon move on to gently pushing against boundaries and testing the waters in a completely normal way. However, there will be a significant minority of children who have had frightening, traumatic and unpredictable experiences with adults. For these children, the prospect of spending long hours with a new teacher will be frightening. They may have heard and believed scary stories about you from their peers, struggle to grasp the expectations around conduct and behaviour in your classroom, fear that you will not like them, that you can't be trusted to respond predictably, or that you will set them work that is too hard for them, and subsequently expend a lot of their energy managing their own anxiety and struggling to understand what is expected of them and how to conform to it.

It is these children who will benefit most from extra effort put into getting to know about them before the year begins. Gather as much information about all the children who will be in your class as you can, and then focus on building up a fuller picture of any whose history suggests that they might need additional support. This includes children with known special educational needs, children who are looked-after or previously looked-after, children with recognised behavioural challenges, and those who are known to live in adverse circumstances.

Information can be gathered from previous teachers (at the child's last school if necessary) and other classroom staff, from planning that has previously been put in place to support them, from SENCOs and designated teachers and from previous assessments of social and emotional needs using, for instance, the Boxall Profile or Fagus (assessment and monitoring tools for social, emotional and behavioural development commonly used in UK schools). A visit to the child's previous school, or their home, may be appropriate but, in any case, the views of parents and carers should be sought as they are most likely to know their child's particular needs. All of this information can help to build up a profile of the child's strengths and weaknesses, and any difficulties that a child has experienced in school and in their lives up to this point.

However, it is never really possible to know exactly how all of this theoretical and anecdotal knowledge will play out once the child is in the classroom with you until that day actually arrives. A child is more than the sum of what is written on their support plan, and knowing that a child has experienced four ACEs does not equate to a rounded description of them as an individual, their personalities, their quirks, their coping mechanisms or their gifts. Begin the year with an open mind, knowledgeable about the children in your class, but without pre-conceived ideas, and then set about getting to know them in person.

Building relationships

In the first weeks with a new class of children, building relationships should be a significant focus. As the teacher, you will be getting to know the children, and they will be getting to know you. There may be a short 'honeymoon period' as children tentatively explore the new environment of your particular classroom, and this is the time to set out routines, reinforce the classroom code of conduct and ensure that all children are aware of your expectations. Establishing a predictable, safe routine as early as possible, accompanied by an understanding but firm response and re-direction when children miss the mark, will be instrumental in helping even anxious children to settle into your class more quickly.

Think about how you welcome children into the classroom. Greeting each child individually with a welcoming smile as they enter may take a little extra time at the start of a lesson, but could pay dividends in terms of time saved settling the class ready for learning. Some children will arrive at the classroom door in a heightened state after a tricky journey through crowded and overwhelming corridors, and this regular greeting could become part of an established routine for a calm beginning to the lesson, as well as a way to make a brief personal connection with each child in the class.

Activities involving the whole class can be used to encourage relationships to form, especially if the children are new to each other as well as new to the teacher. However, be aware that ice-breaker activities can be awkward for many people, especially children who have learned to protect themselves by being as invisible as possible. Instead, try asking all the children to write or draw about their worries or fears about being in a new class, or about their hopes and goals for the year ahead. This can be done during form time for older students, and can be re-visited later in the year to explore whether any of their fears were realised, or to see how close they are to achieving their goals. A few minutes out of the lesson to ask all the children to share information about a fairly neutral topic, such as their favourite food, or the TV show of the moment, can help to break down some barriers and encourage reticent children to participate in a situation where there is relatively little pressure.

During the first few weeks, identify children who are likely to benefit from spending a little extra time with you. For instance, try asking a child to assist you with a simple job for five minutes, such as clearing up after a task, or at break or lunchtime, and use this time for more informal conversations. Repeat this regularly. Make a note of the things they tell you and ask about them later to forge connections. A simple question asking how a child's poorly parent is now, or whether their dog recovered from its operation, will demonstrate to a child that you have their welfare in mind. These informal conversations can help children to develop a more positive view of their interactions with teachers than they might previously have experienced.

Time spent forging appropriate relationships with children is never time wasted. As Paul Dix (2017, p.141) puts it, 'some children follow rules, some follow people'. A child who has broken every rule might go to the ends of the earth for a teacher who shows a genuine interest in them, and deals with them with consistency, fairness and empathy.

Expectations

The start of a new school year is the natural time to state and re-state expectations of children's behaviour and conduct both in the classroom and around school. It is unlikely that expecting children to just 'know' what appropriate behaviour looks like will be an effective long-term strategy, and simple codes of conduct in every classroom can act as general reference points without resorting to lengthy lists of rules for every occasion. However, in any discussion centred on having high and consistent expectations of children, there must also be recognition that some children's starting points on the path towards reaching those expectations are considerably behind others.

In my first term of teaching, I was given a valuable lesson on expectations by a girl in my bottom set Year 7 class. I had asked the whole class a question that they all could have been expected to know the answer to from the activity we had just done, and a forest of hands had shot up. I called on this one girl, and she said, without a trace of humour or cheekiness, 'I got a new rabbit this week.' A few kids sniggered, but I don't believe the girl had any intention to be disruptive. She just looked at me, waiting for my response to her exciting news. Not only had she not grasped the activity we had done, or really listened to the question I was asking, but she, at 11 years old, was offering this information with all the naive excitement of a five-year-old child, completely unaware of the inappropriateness of that statement in that moment.

Children who have missed out on key stages in their development due to early trauma, who have lived in an environment where expectations were not consistent or where adults did not model appropriate behaviour, or who have hidden disabilities such as Foetal Alcohol Spectrum Disorder (FASD), can be socially, emotionally and behaviourally much younger than their chronological age. The social niceties that their peers might take for granted could be completely lacking. They may still exhibit toddler behaviours, such as snatching, interrupting, speaking in non sequiturs, responding to provocation by physical means and expressing negative emotions through crying or angry outbursts. Building in the missing stages of their development can be long and patient work and, especially for children experiencing the lifelong impact of pre-natal alcohol exposure, expectations will need to be explicitly taught and re-taught, along with concrete strategies to help them meet those expectations. As you lay out your expectations for behaviour and conduct at the start of the new school year, be aware of those children for whom the goal of meeting your expectations is still a distant dot on the horizon.

Effective interventions and support from the start

For many children, internal motivation, desire to conform to the group norm, and a consistent system of rewards and sanctions will work together to ensure behaviour and conduct that is largely appropriate. For those children who do not seem to respond to these systems, it is often only after long cycles of misdemeanour followed by sanction, followed by further misdemeanours and an escalation of sanctions, that alternative approaches are attempted. In a trauma- and attachment-aware classroom, the adults act as behaviour detectives, always looking at what drives the unwanted behaviour so that strategies can address the causes of challenging behaviour and not only the results.

Investigating the root causes of a child's behaviour takes time, but so does filling in incident forms, arranging meeting after meeting with senior staff, and administering detentions. Armed with the information gathered at the start of the school year, and the relationships that have been developed with students, the trauma-informed teacher can aim to get the most appropriate interventions and support in place right from the start, so that the rest of the school year can be focused more on learning, and less on managing challenging behaviour.

It is perhaps most helpful to illustrate this approach by considering individual children.

> Katie struggles to organise herself. She often forgets or loses essential equipment, and repeatedly turns up to class with no pens, or missing her books. She struggles to stay focused on tasks, and often hands her homework in late or not at all.

A child like Katie may receive many sanctions over the course of a school year for her lack of equipment or missing homework, but they might have little or no effect if the root cause of her difficulties is poor executive functioning skills. Visual planners, stepped instructions, checklists, and the use of writing frames and other scaffolding techniques can all be used to support Katie to meet expectations.

> James constantly shouts out in class, draws attention to himself, monopolises his teacher's time, and interrupts others. He asks trivial questions and always seems to have something to say. Sometimes he sings or makes silly noises when he should be quietly working.

Children who incessantly attract the teacher's attention can be draining. They may appear to be playing the role of the class clown, or attention-seeking. However, it is possible that James is displaying attachment-seeking behaviour. He may have a poor grasp of the concept of permanency, and therefore experiences being left at the school gate by his carer as an act of abandonment. He feels unsafe and insecure and, to compensate, seeks desperately to make attachments with any adult who is available in the only way he knows how. James needs attention, but this can be given in a way that is in the teacher's control, such as seating him in the teacher's direct eyeline and giving positive attention throughout the lesson such as a smile or a thumbs-up. Giving an attachment-seeking child the attention they crave is not the same as giving in to their behaviour. In fact, ignoring James, or keeping him at a distance, will only exacerbate his behaviour as it is rooted in fear of being forgotten or ignored.

> Alfie is constantly on the move. He runs everywhere and crashes around, even banging himself on furniture or other children. During playtime, he sometimes plays roughly and children have been hurt. In the classroom he fidgets and wriggles on his seat, and he can't seem to stand still in the dinner queue.

Alfie is likely to quickly become the subject of whispered conversations between parents at the school gates. He is 'that child': the one that the other parents want their children to be protected from. Yet rather than being an out-of-control child who does not know how to behave, it is possible that Alfie has difficulties processing sensory information and, as a result, is pushing, crashing, running and moving in order to give his body the sensory input it craves. Fiddle toys, wobble cushions, and regular activity breaks such as pushing or carrying heavy objects might give his body proprioceptive feedback and lessen his sensory-seeking behaviour.

> Scarlett hardly ever speaks at school. She does not raise her hand to answer questions, sits silently during group activities, and seems to have few friends. Her work is adequate, she is making progress, and she is generally well-behaved, but she has frequent absences from school, and her parents report that she has trouble sleeping at night, has regular meltdowns and often refuses to come to school.

Scarlett is the sort of child who could easily slip under the radar in a busy classroom. She does not cause any trouble or draw attention to herself, and she apparently gets on with her work without needing any help. Yet there seems to be a discrepancy between what the school sees and what her parents report. This is always worth investigating further. A conversation with her adoptive parents may reveal that Scarlett has attachment difficulties. She is exhibiting anxious/avoidant attachment behaviours at school, trying to be invisible as a way to ensure her own safety. Even if she doesn't understand her work, she is unlikely to attract attention to herself by asking for help. However, stress is building up under the surface, and this can erupt once she is at home around adults with whom she feels safe. She may seem 'fine' at school, but could simply be masking her distress, and so could benefit from a key adult to act as an attachment figure, involvement in nurture groups and buddying schemes, and a pro-active approach to ensuring that her basic needs are being met throughout the day. A child like Scarlett would rather go thirsty for hours than ask for a drink of water.

> Kyle is bossy and rude to both adults and children and seems to have an opinion on everything. Other children don't like to work with him because he orders them around so much and interferes with what they are doing. He always has to be in charge, and everyone has to do things his way.

Controlling behaviour like Kyle's can be disruptive and difficult to manage, but it is often rooted in fear rather than defiance or a desire to feel superior. This fear may be rooted in a deep lack of trust in the ability of adults to keep him safe, or linked to anxiety around specific events such as transitions. One approach is to demonstrate to Kyle that the teacher is actually firmly in control through establishing clear and explicit boundaries around distribution of responsibilities, issues such as where children will sit, or who will be in charge of each aspect of a task or group activity. These well-defined boundaries can support a child like Kyle to feel safe as he will see that the adults do know what they are doing. At the same time as taking control away from Kyle in decisions that should be made by the teacher, control can be given back to him in a measured way, for instance by allowing him some choice of activity, giving him some agency over the way he chooses to complete a particular task, or assigning him a role of some importance that will not impact too much on the other children, such as watering the plants in the classroom.

It is pointless for everybody involved to waste time implementing strategies that will not work, because they do nothing to address the root causes of the behaviour. Making a commitment at the start of the year to move quickly past the 'what' of unwanted behaviour, and instead to get to the 'why' of it, will save a lot of time, energy and heartache in the long run.

BENJAMIN ADLARD PRIMARY SCHOOL

Towards a fresh start for struggling children

Situated in a deprived area, with a high level of housing instability, Benjamin Adlard Primary School has had to become very adept at quickly settling in new students. The 240-pupil school has a turnaround of approximately 30 per cent of its student population each year and, of the current Year 6 class, only six have been in the school since Reception.

Many families move into the area because they are attracted from large cities by the relatively cheap and readily available rented housing. Some are escaping debt problems, domestic violence and social problems. Benjamin Adlard welcomes children undergoing managed moves from other schools, who have been excluded or are at risk of exclusion, or who have been out of school for some time. The school also serves a small, but stable, traveller community, and has a women's refuge in its catchment area.

Members of staff from the school meet the family of every child transferring into the school mid-year and gather as much information as possible, not only about the child's academic history, but also about them as a person, what their likes and dislikes are, what they like to be called, and whether they have any previous issues around behaviour. If the child is not out of education, the previous primary school will also be contacted. There is an emphasis on building relationships before the child's first day. Each child will be taken to meet their class teacher, and the other children in their class. The students will be asked to raise their hands if they were also new this year, in a visual display that this latest new child will not be alone in their experience. A 'buddy' system ensures that each new arrival already has a relationship with at least one other child in their class.

Benjamin Adlard works in partnership with other schools from more affluent areas to create a bank of free, quality uniform items for new starters. Partner schools donate unwanted uniform, and staff at Benjamin Adlard wash and prepare each item ready for new arrivals. Students can be provided with clothes, trainers, PE [Physical Education] kit, bags, coats and whatever else they need, so that they can start on their first day fully equipped. This takes the pressure off newly arrived families who may not be financially able to commit to the cost of an entire new uniform. The school is also part of the 'Magic Breakfasts' scheme, so new arrivals are offered a small supply of surplus cereals and bagels donated by the scheme to ensure that, at least for their first few days, the children will arrive at school having had a good breakfast. Even before their first day, children and families know that Benjamin Adlard is a school that cares about them, and about their welfare.

Every child at Benjamin Adlard is part of a 'team', and new arrivals are given their team badge before they start. Each child also wears a gold star as a reminder of the school's Golden Rules, and this is also presented to new arrivals before their first day to welcome them to the community, and to act as a reminder of the ethos the school is creating.

On their first day, new starters avoid the daunting crowding and noise of the playground full of strangers and are instead taken straight to the main entrance where they are met by the head teacher. Baseline assessments are left until after the child has been at the school for at least a fortnight, so that they are more settled and more ready to do their best.

Consistency of expectations across the school is foundational to ensuring that children settle quickly to Benjamin Adlard's routines. New arrivals see other children modelling expected behaviour from the very first day, and soon recognise what is expected of them. This includes outside of lessons, where students, for instance, walk on the left in the corridors, and hold the doors open for each other and members of staff. Head teacher, Sam Coy, views such simple actions as providing multiple opportunities for positive interactions between students and staff throughout the day.

For children who have particular difficulties in settling into the classroom environment, Benjamin Adlard has a forest school [outdoor, hands-on learning in the natural environment in all weathers] . Here, children can experience overcoming adversity and building resilience in a less high-stakes situation. One new arrival spent most of his day in the forest school at the beginning of his time at the school, and could only manage ten minutes a day in the classroom. Now he is fully integrated with his peers and making excellent progress.

Like many schools which espouse a trauma-informed approach, Benjamin Adlard seeks individualised solutions to each individual child's difficulties. Sam Coy sees these as learning opportunities for all students: 'I explain to all the pupils that this particular child has extra support during assemblies because they find assemblies hard, while another child might have extra support during Maths because they find

Maths hard. Every child knows that if they have a need, the school will try to support it, but they all have different needs. All the students can understand this reasoning.' One example was a boy who was really struggling with the crowded cloakroom, and was responding by hitting out and hurting people. Now that child hangs his coat in the head teacher's office, and benefits from a little 1–1 time with a trusted adult first thing every morning. Instead of arriving in class full of anxiety, he now arrives settled and ready to learn.

Support for all children does not end once their transition period is over and they have settled into their classes. The school has a lunchtime club focused on nurture, building social skills, and reflective and restorative practice, and uses a reward system based on ideas supplied by the children themselves, such as a hot chocolate with the head teacher. A dedicated staff team puts a lot of work into EHCP[1] applications for children who have additional needs, including social, emotional and mental health needs. Sam feels that having an EHCP put in place is essential as some children who manage well in the relatively small and nurturing environment of primary school can flounder in secondary school if the support structure for them is not put in place early. A full-time family support worker is employed by the school, and links with local higher education providers allow them to take student social workers on placement to support children and families where appropriate.

The success of Benjamin Adlard's approach is measurable. In a school with 70 per cent of children entitled to free school meals, and 40 per cent SEND, fixed-term exclusions have fallen from over 40, four years ago, to zero last year, and the school's Ofsted grading[2] has risen rapidly from Inadequate in 2014 to Good in 2016, noting that 'Outcomes for pupils are improving rapidly'. This improvement is, in large part, down to the dedicated staff team who, under new headship, have worked together to transform the culture and ethos of the school.

---

1   Education, Health and Care Plans describe children's special educational needs and the support they will receive. They are legal documents prepared by Local Authorities for children who need more support than their educational setting usually provides.

2   Ofsted is the body in England that inspects educational settings. Settings are graded on a 4-point scale: Inadequate; Requires Improvement; Good; Outstanding.

Chapter 6

REWARDS AND CONSEQUENCES

In this chapter:

Systems of escalating consequences

Time out, detentions, internal and external exclusions

Public behaviour tracking and classroom wall charts

Praise and rewards

Whether it's the certificate for good attendance, or the detention for failure to complete homework, most schools operate within a system of rewards for desired behaviour and consequences for behaviour that does not meet the requirements of the school. Maintaining high standards of behaviour and readiness to learn is important for everyone, including children who have experienced trauma. Schools are complex systems which must somehow be made to work for hundreds, sometimes thousands of individuals who walk through their doors every day. However, traditional models of managing behaviour may have unexpected and unwanted results when children are affected by complex trauma and attachment difficulties.

Systems of escalating consequences

Common in many schools, these systems are designed to ensure that everyone knows the desired behaviour, and is aware of the consequences of not meeting the standard. They usually follow a ladder of consequences beginning with, for instance, a verbal warning, and escalating with each repeat of the unwanted behaviour.

Such systems make several assumptions about the children who are affected by them. The first is that the child knows how to behave. In reality, knowing how to behave is no simple task, even for children who have been raised in secure and nurturing environments. Schools are not like homes, and each teacher, each classroom, each school setting, will have its own, often unspoken, code of behaviour for children to master. It is like suddenly being faced with a multi-course place setting at a Buckingham Palace dinner and expecting a child to just know which knife and fork to use. Paul Dix (2017, p.22) calls the idea that children should just know how to behave 'an unrealistic expectation' that 'plays havoc with your ability to manage the behaviour in front of you'. He goes on to explain that children need to be explicitly taught expected behaviours, and this should be reiterated frequently. Just as we don't teach children to read by giving them a book and giving them detention if they don't read it, expected behaviour also needs to be explicitly taught from the bottom up. Telling a child to 'behave', or 'settle down', will have little effect if the child in question doesn't understand the specific behaviours being asked for.

It is tempting to solve this problem by devising ever more complex codes and rules to cover every possible eventuality, but this creates problems of its own. Neither students nor teachers can reliably be expected to remember every detail of every sub-section of a code of conduct that makes *War and Peace* look like a novella by comparison, and inconsistency is bound to creep in, undermining the very purpose of the system.

> The most difficult thing is to try and get consistency across all lessons with all staff. The boundaries, approaches, strategies and behaviour management change from class to class, making it even harder for children like mine, who are anxious already, or who struggle to identify what is expected of them.

The second assumption inherent in consequence models is that the child is able to meet the behavioural requirement, but is choosing not to for some reason. Rewards and consequences are rooted in the behaviourist model of learning which assumes that children are essentially blank slates, ready to learn through positive and negative reinforcement. In reality, all teachers will know that there are no blank slates. Children arrive on their first day at school complete with a lifetime of experiences, all of which will impact on their ability to learn, behave, cope, relate and thrive in the school environment. For some children, this is complicated by the presence of additional needs, which may as yet be undiagnosed. Children who have experienced traumatic early lives, multiple adverse childhood experiences, insecure attachments, and loss, may already be on a very different trajectory from those who have been raised in a secure, nurturing home, even at the age of four years old. Without intervention, the gap between these children and their peers can only be expected to widen as they progress through the school system.

Children do, of course, learn from positive and negative reinforcement. They also experience 'social learning' as they observe the behaviour of their peers and the adults in their lives. However, as Gore Langton and Boy (2017) observe, children who have experienced trauma may well have learned different things in their early lives than their peers. Stealing food, for instance, is a well-adapted behaviour in an environment where the adults don't provide meals. When children are removed from environments where these behaviours made perfect sense, and placed in an environment where they don't, the children appear difficult and challenging. The behaviours which have served them well in one place, are likely to land them in trouble in another.

Unwanted behaviours may be driven by underlying difficulties. A hyper-vigilant child, primed to be on the alert for danger by years of living in an environment of domestic violence, may well be easily distracted in a busy classroom, fall behind with their work, and distract others. Can they control this behaviour? Some may be able to some of the time, but it will take valuable internal resources that will then not be available for learning. Other underlying causes of unwanted behaviour that are common in children who have experienced trauma might include:

- Heightened anxiety and poor ability to regulate stress responses leaving children likely to jump to fight–flight–freeze responses

- Attention difficulties

- Neurological damage caused by Foetal Alcohol Spectrum Disorder (FASD)

- Difficulties with impulse control

- Poor executive functioning skills

- Fear: of there not being enough to go around, of not being able to do what the teacher asks, of being humiliated

- Attachment-seeking behaviour, such as calling out, making noise, being clingy, and otherwise attracting attention

- Frustration arising from speech, language and communication difficulties

- Sensory processing difficulties leading to overwhelm, or sensory-seeking behaviour.

Children with FASD can be particularly immune to behaviour systems designed around consequences and rewards. FASD affects a child's cognitive abilities, their memory and their ability to maintain their attention on the task, meaning that children with this condition may often feel confused or overwhelmed. Without support, feelings of low self-esteem and a sense of failure may be added to the mix. Some children with variants of FASD have an average or above average IQ, which makes their behavioural struggles even more likely to appear to be caused by laziness or defiance. Regardless of their academic abilities, children with FASD will struggle with adaptive behaviour and have difficulties communicating their needs. Their failure to meet expected norms of behaviour must be seen in the context of their disability. For a child with FASD who struggles with difficulties generalising and understanding abstract concepts, coupled with a lack of cause-and-effect thinking, rewards-and-consequences systems are unlikely to ever result in improvements.

When a child's behaviour falls short of our expectations, especially if this is out of character, or is persistent but the usual approaches seem to have no effect, there are questions that need to be asked. Does this child truly understand what is expected? Is this child able to meet the expectation? If not, could they learn if explicitly taught, or do reasonable adjustments need to be made? Recognising that a child's behaviour may have underlying causes that need to be addressed is not the same as allowing the child's behaviour to continue unchecked. It is about recognising that the journey towards the desired behaviour may be a longer and more winding one for this child than for others, and then putting in place the support they need to complete it. The oft-repeated sentiment that consequences are a part of life and as adults we can't expect to escape them does hold some truth, which makes it all the more vital that we understand the behaviour of our most challenging children. 'Demanding that children be able to do now what we would like them to be able to do in the future does not make our wishes come true' (Gore Langton and Boy, 2017, p.106).

The idea that behaviour is communication is gaining currency among educators, but how does this theory help us in a busy classroom where there are 30 different sets of, sometimes competing, needs and communications? In some ways, it does not help. Classroom strategies will only go so far if they are not supported by whole-school approaches. If Keiran is about to throw a chair, then the safety of the other people in the vicinity must be paramount. While the teacher may well be aware that Keiran's chair throwing is communication, it's not always possible to stop everything and listen to what he is saying. This is where the systems surrounding the class teacher become so important. Keiran must be stopped, for his own sake and for the sake of others. But understanding what happened before that incident, and the decision about what will happen after, will be crucial to determining whether Keiran will end up on a fast track to exclusion, or be able to remain in school, and eventually thrive.

> I spent half an hour one Monday morning talking to a Year 9 student who had been taken into foster care over the weekend. He was a mess, obviously. Later that day, he was in my lesson, being disruptive. It was nothing new, only the same low-level disruptive behaviour I was used to from him – calling out, singing loudly, interrupting – but the other students started complaining, saying he was stopping them from working. Our school had a very rigid behaviour policy with sanctions at every level. There was no calm-down zone or anything similar. If I followed the policy, he would end up in detention. It was the last thing he needed.

'No excuses' approaches to behaviour management risk becoming inflexible, and leaving no wiggle room for situations where an alternative approach might yield better results. For children who have experienced traumatic early lives, carefully structured escalating systems of consequences may have little effect, or even promote the very behaviour they are designed to reduce, for a number of reasons:

- Lack of cause-and-effect thinking – The child is unable to link the positive and negative consequences meaningfully to the behaviour that triggered them, so never seems to learn from the reinforcement.

- The child's negative view of themselves is reinforced by the system, rather than reduced, and they may seek to further confirm that through continuing unwanted behaviour.

- Resentment grows, especially if the child feels as though the consequence was unfair.

- For children with difficulties caused by attachment problems and relational trauma, it can cause a breach of trust, damaging whatever relationship existed.

- Some children have experienced such traumatic events that even the worst sanctions a school can deploy are no deterrent to them – being excluded from school is no match for losing your whole family.

- Children who are repeatedly cycling through the consequences system may gain a certain notoriety and welcome the brief moment of fame and attention this gives them.

- For children who have learned that becoming invisible is their best route to survival, the existence of these systems can cause anxiety and fear, even if the sanctions are never applied to them.

Maintaining high standards of behaviour in school is important for every member of the school community. If behaviour is poor, nobody is learning, including traumatised children. In fact, routine, structure and predictability are crucial for these most challenged and challenging children. However, approaches which prioritise relationships, safety and nurture, which take into account the sometimes complex drivers of poor behaviour, and which respond accordingly, are likely to have better results long term than applying a tick list of consequences regardless of the circumstances. If the same children are always in detention, always outside someone's office, always on the rain cloud or red traffic light, then the current system is not working for them, or anybody else.

Approaches to try

- Use natural consequences wherever possible as these will support development of cause-and-effect thinking.

- Liaise with parents and carers to build up a profile of the child's strengths, difficulties and triggers, and ensure that this is shared with relevant staff to give them the information they need to head off challenging behaviour before it begins where possible.

- As far as possible, replace consequences with supportive interventions designed to encourage and enable the child towards the desired behaviour.

- Pick your battles. It is better (and less draining for everyone) to make real progress with one or two serious difficulties than to make little or no progress in every single thing.

- Review any behaviour or pastoral plans to ensure that they offer more than a list of required behaviours and consequences for infraction. Each child's plan should take account of their particular needs and offer a clear, supported path towards achieving the progress that is hoped for.

- Key adults can work with children to support them in understanding the impact of their behaviour on other children, and to explore alternative ways of expressing their needs or emotions.

- Long lists of rules are difficult to remember. Create a short code of conduct (preferably with input from students) to display on every classroom wall, and draw attention to it regularly, exploring what terms like 'Respect each other' might look like in practice. Refer to this code when praising and correcting students.

- If there are specific rules for your teaching area (e.g. a technology room) ensure that these are referred to and explained frequently, and permanently displayed, preferably with visuals to support instant understanding.

Time out, detentions, internal and external exclusions

My daughter was once isolated in an office, screaming 'Don't leave me alone!' She was six at the time, and the head would not let anyone go in to her because they would be 'rewarding her bad behaviour'!

For children who need safe attachment relationships and the security of predictable structures and routines, methods of dealing with challenging behaviour that remove the child from their safe relationships, and upset the predictability of their routine are counter-productive. Remember that many traumatised children have experienced several losses of home and family, which they may have internalised as rejections which reflect badly on them as a person. It is not hard to see the reinforcement of that negative self-image involved in sending them away as a punishment, whether for a time out, an internal exclusion or a fixed-period exclusion. If a child is already falling behind their peers or struggling to learn because of an underlying special educational need or disability, then being removed regularly from the opportunity to learn will not improve that situation either.

Removing a child may provide temporary relief for everyone else, but, unless it is accompanied by genuine supportive interventions, it will solve nothing for the child, and merely postpones the problem or, in the case of permanent exclusion, moves it somewhere else. In situations where removing a child from the classroom is absolutely necessary, then serious thought must be given to where that child is being removed *to* as well as where they are being removed *from*. Children and young people who are unable to regulate themselves with the help of a supportive adult in the classroom are unlikely to be able to do so alone on a chair in the corridor outside the head teacher's office.

Inclusion matters. Children who are included gain a sense of belonging to the school community, which pays dividends in terms of engagement and subsequently achievement. Repeatedly excluding children from the classroom or school limits their ability to form meaningful relationships, disengages them from the community, and limits their access to learning.

Detentions at break times and lunchtimes can have a similar effect. We give children breaks from sitting in the classroom for a reason. Children with sensory challenges, in particular, will benefit from the sensory break that a run around the playground provides, and all children have an opportunity to develop and learn social skills and navigate friendships in the spaces between formal learning. These are valuable skills that children with challenging behaviour often need support to improve. Removing the opportunity to mix with their peers will not help them in this task.

When he was in Year 4, my foster son had a detention at lunchtime at least once each week. The reason was always the same: disruptive behaviour in the dinner queue. He could tell me what behaviour was expected, but somehow he couldn't seem to stick to it in the moment. I spoke to his teacher about his severe food anxiety, and suggested that he might be fighting to get to the front of the queue so that he could be sure that he'd get some food. She talked to the other children and said, 'From now on, Alex is always first in the queue.' There were no more disruptions, and no more detentions. By the time he got into Year 6, he no longer needed to be first in the queue, and could queue with the other children safely.

After-school detentions are designed to disrupt a student's intended routine. Instead of going home with their peers, or having that extra hour of free time, they will stay behind in school. If frequent, detentions can inhibit a child's availability for extra-curricular activities which are important for developing that vital sense of belonging in the school community, and reduce the time available to complete homework, which some children may struggle to complete within a reasonable time frame in the first place.

We have seen already how children with a background of trauma need routine, stability and predictability in order to maximise their sense of safety. Many adoptive parents and foster carers serve predictable food, follow predictable routines for bedtimes, holiday in the same places every year, and even create daily plans for the school holidays. After-school detention disrupts any predictable routine around the end of the school day, which, as we will see in Chapter 7, is a transition time that can often be a flashpoint. Children with additional needs and executive functioning difficulties are often not ready to travel home from school alone, even at secondary school age, meaning that parents need to re-organise their plans for picking up, which can be complex if there are other children to consider.

All of this would, perhaps, pale into insignificance if time outs, detentions and exclusions had the desired effect on the most challenging students. They may well act as a deterrent for children who would most likely be inclined to conform anyway, but if an audit of your school's disciplinary procedures shows the same children's names appearing on detention lists time and time again, then although they may satisfy our desire for punishment for infractions, they are clearly not accomplishing anything in terms of improving the child's behaviour and ensuring those same infractions do not occur again in the future.

Approaches to try

- Ensure that disciplinary policies balance accountability with an understanding of behaviours rooted in trauma, and that there is a clear, supported pathway to enable struggling children to reach desired standards.

- Create spaces within the classroom for a child to use to calm down, rather than using time out.

- Have a safe space or safe person a child can access if they are escalating and need to leave the classroom. This is not a sterile 'inclusion room', but a genuine calm-down zone or nurture room, staffed by key adults who are pro-active in supporting children with strategies to become regulated so that they can return to learning at the earliest opportunity.

- Communicate with parents and carers around issues such as uniform, persistent lateness and homework problems, and agree a plan of support.

- Focus on immediate responses that prioritise relationships – a two-minute conversation at the end of the class is likely to be more effective than a one-hour detention a week later.

- Replace internal exclusion or detention with time spent carrying out a meaningful activity with a key adult, preferably something that contributes to the school community – time in beats time out.

- Instead of sending a child to senior staff for a lecture or sanctions, invite the senior staff member to sit in the room in an observational (not confrontational) capacity as you speak to the child. This way, the support of senior leadership is visible, but the matter is resolved within the relationship between the class teacher and the student.

- Prioritise natural consequences and restorative actions. Paul Dix (2017) outlines a simple five-step restorative process in his book, *When the Adults Change, Everything Changes*.

- Be prepared to delay making a decision about consequences if emotions are running high.

- Avoid being drawn into escalation over secondary behaviours. If you ask the student to hand over their forbidden electronic device and they drag their feet on the way to your desk, the important thing is that the device is handed over, as per your request.

Public behaviour tracking and classroom wall charts

Whether it's elaborately constructed displays of sunshine and rain clouds, or something as simple as names on the board, it seems as though almost every classroom in the land features some version of visual and public behaviour tracking.

I was taught the 'name on the board' method as a trainee. It was presented as a strategy that would reduce the time spent on negative talk in the classroom. Instead of interrupting the lesson to correct a child, simply write their name on the board, and carry on. I could see the sense in that, and used it enthusiastically in my first teaching job until one day, on turning round from the board, I noticed that the child whose name I had just written was grinning at his friend and doing what can only be described as a fist pump.

Wall charts and similar displays rely on the assumption that the child both knows how to behave, and is capable of achieving the desired behaviour. If we assume that the answer to both of these questions is 'yes', then the child surely only needs to be motivated properly to want to behave correctly, and reminded occasionally if their behaviour slips. Theoretically, the wall chart fulfils both of these functions.

If only things were so simple. In reality, most children are not lacking in internal motivation to connect, to fit in and to 'please'. For those who succeed, the external motivation is simply icing on the cake, confirming their positive view of themselves and the world. For those who fail, the public reinforcement of their failure damages their view of themselves, creates doubt about their worth and quenches their internal motivation. If a child is unable, for whatever reason, to do what we are expecting of them, then our best efforts to motivate them will have the opposite effect. For children whose view of themselves has been coloured by early trauma, these strategies can fail in surprising ways.

Think about Amy. Amy is almost always on the sunshine. In fact, remaining on the sunshine is the primary aim of each day. The mere thought of slipping down the chart creates a knot of dread in the pit of her stomach. She works hard every day to be compliant, to ensure the teacher knows that she is being 'good', so much so that her teacher thinks she's an attention-seeker. Amy has learned that to be safe, she needs to be good, so that adults will like her and take care of her. For Amy, losing her place under the sun means much more than a temporary change of status; her desperate need to be approved of is a survival mechanism ingrained in her from her earliest years. Amy's behaviour is perfect, but overwhelming anxiety means her work is suffering, and her parents say that she doesn't sleep at night, cries every day before school and says she doesn't want to go.

Then there's James. James struggles to meet behaviour expectations, but he does try his best to keep his name in the right places on the chart. After a good week, an unfortunate incident on Friday afternoon results in his name dropping down a level. James kicks off, shouting and angry. This results in further consequences. For James, this public display of his failure ignites an overwhelming sense of shame. Unable to deal with these strong negative emotions, he responds by attacking their source in a defensive rage.

Finally, we have Chloe. Chloe's name is always on the board, under the rain cloud, against the red traffic light. She doesn't seem to care about it. In fact, she lays bets with her friends about how many consecutive days she can stay in the 'naughty zone'. Chloe has given up hope of ever living in the sunshine, but she still wants to feel good about herself and mask her sense of shame, so she subverts the system. At last she is 'somebody': famous among her peers.

Amy needs to feel safe, connected and noticed in a way that is not linked to behaviour. Her good behaviour can still be rewarded in quieter, more private ways, but the wall chart is reinforcing her core view that she is worthless if she is not perfect. James needs reassurance that an incidence of bad behaviour does not cancel out all of his previous good behaviour, and that even though we all fail sometimes, it doesn't make us failures. Chloe needs to be cut off from the oxygen of public recognition of her misdemeanours so that bravado becomes pointless, and then supported, quietly and privately, to re-invent her school persona.

Paul Dix (2017, p.21) describes behaviour charts as techniques that are 'left over from an age where children being shamed in public was thought to be edifying'. If we had such charts on the walls of our staffrooms, how would it affect our approach to our jobs? As an adult, seeing our names at the bottom of the list might motivate us to some extent. A strong and confident person might take bold steps to ensure that never happened again. But it might also cause embarrassment and shame. How would we deal with that? Would we hide away, become defensive, make light of it by joking, or become angry and resentful? What if someone's work had suffered that term because of circumstances beyond their control? Would they feel unfairly singled out? And how would we feel about that one staff member with few commitments outside of school, who makes every meeting, completes every task and always sits smugly under the sunshine, seemingly effortlessly? Does your school's staff disciplinary procedure include a stage where you are publicly called out on your failures in front of the whole staffroom?

> The behaviour system of traffic lights does not work for my child and the school insist on using it. I have sat in front of the school Head and both cried and begged her not to use it and she has ignored me and told me it works. My son has consistently missed end of term treat day and been heartbroken.

Moving towards a system that is more trauma- and attachment-aware, and focuses on supporting children towards acceptable behaviour within the context of trusting relationships, does not mean abandoning boundaries and encouraging a free-for-all. Boundaries must be secure and steadfast, but the methods by which we ensure children stay within them should be flexible, compassionate and designed to build them up, not shame and humiliate them. As Gore Langton and Boy (2017, p.32) put it, 'It is difficult to think of children who will *not* benefit from a school that is more focused on providing attuned, high-quality relationships...and on flexibly meeting children's needs.'

Approaches to try

- As far as possible, seek to correct behaviour and apply consequences in private.

- Keep the positive and negative consequences related to behaviour separate – one doesn't cancel out the other.

- Make the most of your 'presence' in the classroom, using non-verbal cues to acknowledge positives, and act as reminders. A thumbs-up or a smile recognises a student's achievement just as much as a name under a sunshine. A meaningful look or a quick shake of the head can sometimes be enough to stop disruptive behaviour in its tracks without disrupting the flow of the lesson.

- Instead of a behaviour chart, display your simple classroom code of conduct on the wall, and refer to it regularly. If an individual student is, say, talking or fidgeting, remind the whole class of the part of the code of conduct that relates to sitting quietly and listening, and offer praise to those who are achieving the desired behaviour.

- When speaking individually to a child in private, refer to the code of conduct, reminding them of the expectations.

- For individual children with particular and intractable difficulties, create a personalised plan that is not focused on the behaviour, but on recognising when the child uses a taught strategy to avoid the unwanted behaviour, for example recognising when the child raises their hand instead of calling out, or when they use a fiddle object instead of fidgeting and disrupting others.

Praise and rewards

For children whose internal view of themselves is affected by trauma, neglect and abuse, praise and rewards can be difficult to handle. The success of reward charts as motivation relies on children having secure cause-and-effect thinking and recognising how their choices have directly resulted in that reward. If cause-and-effect thinking is undeveloped, then children will find such charts confusing and potentially perceive them as unfair. Like most behaviourist strategies, reward charts assume that children understand what is required and have the ability to achieve it, but just lack the proper motivation. Parents often use star charts as an aid to toilet training their toddlers, but expecting a six-month-old baby to earn stickers for using the potty would be ridiculous, cruel even. Any target or goal setting must take into account the developmental ability of the child to manage the desired behaviour or activity. If not, then the motivational reward system becomes incredibly de-motivating.

Systems where rewards are earned collectively, or results are displayed publicly run into the same difficulties as public behaviour tracking systems. They can be a source of huge shame for children who are continually and visibly falling behind their peers, and where the actions of one child can lead to negative consequences for the whole class, the possibility of bullying and shaming by peers is very real.

Some systems lend themselves to 'gaming', rewarding those children who are most visible for even the smallest of efforts, while leaving those children who quietly get on with their work unrewarded. It is extremely difficult to maintain a whole-school system of merits, house points or rewards in a consistent and fair way. Children notice when things aren't fair.

Some may respond by working the system to their maximum advantage, while others may resent what they perceive as lack of consistency, and kick against the whole system. Rewards for achievements that are not within the child's control are particularly problematic. For instance, awards for good attendance are often impossible to achieve for children with medical difficulties, or other legitimate reasons for missing school. It is surely demoralising for a child in that situation to see other children receiving certificates and prizes for having had the good luck to be healthy.

> My son is receiving post-adoption support to help his anger and insecurity issues. The school say that they agree that missing an afternoon of school a week for this is important and yet we are still sent the upsetting standard letters about his poor attendance, which I feel damage my relationship with the school.

Of course, adults do not praise or reward children only in order to motivate them. Often we simply wish to recognise children's achievements in a tangible way. However, when children have extremely negative internal views of themselves, praise and rewards can be misinterpreted as they go so completely against what the child believes to be true.

A child who believes himself to be a bad, worthless failure will only have this reinforced if he sees other children racing ahead of him on the sticker chart. Conversely, if he does receive rewards and praise, this conflicts with his view of himself so sharply that he may respond by proving just how bad and worthless he is so that the natural order, as he sees it, is restored. For children whose view of themselves is so damaged, praise does not necessarily increase self-esteem. Rather, it can give the child the impression that the teacher praising them is lying, tricking them or just plain gullible. Children whose behaviour is most challenging are most likely to be praised effusively for the smallest improvement. Most of the time these children know that such a high level of praise is not really merited. It devalues the whole currency of praise.

Approaches to try

- Instead of handing out merits or stars or stickers, try a simple 'Well done' accompanied by a smile and maybe even a thumbs-up. It's more personal and more rooted in relationship than any reward chart.

- Ensure that your level of praise is appropriate for the situation, and resist the temptation to praise effusively for the slightest effort from the most challenging student. Muted praise that focuses on specifics works well.

- Build treats and enrichment activities into your schedule that don't need to be earned by exemplary behaviour.

- Make any goals short-term and very specific. Once a child realises that they have no hope of achieving a long-term goal (for example, the 98 per cent attendance required for inclusion in the end of year trip), then is it tempting for them to give up altogether.

- Teachers are often encouraged to correct in private and praise in public, but public praise can be difficult for some children for the reasons outlined above. Instead try a quiet word after class, a postcard home, or a note in the child's book or planner.

- Similarly, if a child is to be recognised in a rewards assembly or similar, ensure that parents and carers are informed in advance so that the child is prepared for the event. It may be more appropriate for some children to spare them the public gaze, however much they deserve the reward.

- Ensure that rewards and consequences are kept separate, and that rewards already earned are not cancelled because of subsequent misdemeanours.

COLEBOURNE PRIMARY SCHOOL
Towards a trauma-informed behaviour policy

At 420-pupil Colebourne Primary, there are no behaviour charts on classroom walls, no escalating systems of consequences, and all staff follow a whole-school policy of no shouting and no shaming. The school's movement towards an attachment- and trauma-aware approach is spear-headed by head teacher and adoptive parent Stuart Guest, and underpinned by a dedicated and well-trained staff team who are united in understanding that children's emotional needs and academic needs are not mutually exclusive.

The school's successful approach goes way beyond re-writing their behaviour policy, and includes an emphasis on staff training and support, commitment to working closely with parents, the development of a dedicated pastoral team, and provision of additional support during unstructured time, such as the pastoral room and the chill-out teepee.

However, the school's way of thinking about behaviour is fundamental to this approach. The behaviour policy is headed with the quote, 'Thinking of a child as behaving badly disposes you to think of punishment. Thinking of a child as struggling to handle something difficult encourages you to help them through their distress,' and goes on to provide a framework within which high expectations can be maintained, safety and relationships are prioritised, and fairness and consistency are promoted, while taking into account children's individual needs.

There is a clear pathway for classroom staff to follow if a child's behaviour is inappropriate, but this pathway is focused on re-direction and support, rather than applying sanctions. Learning mentors and members of the senior leadership team are on hand should a child continue to disrupt in the classroom. Responses are tailored to the situation and the individual child but, for example, a child who has damaged or defaced property would be expected to participate in a 'natural reparation' by repairing the damage, or clearing up the mess. Children are supported to have opportunity to reflect on their actions and the impact this may have had on others and, where appropriate, can show 'sorry' through words and actions.

The whole school uses a behaviour tracking system where members of staff log behavioural incidents on a daily tracking sheet, which are then transferred to a central electronic tracking system. The inclusion team reviews this data weekly, allowing them to spot patterns of difficulties and devise appropriate responses. For instance, behaviour tracking highlighted that there were a significant number of incidents during unstructured times, prompting the introduction of extra staffing and support at playtime and lunchtime. Incidents during these times decreased dramatically as a result. The tracking also allows staff to provide tailored support to individual children as it allows them to see if there are any times in the day or week when incidents are most likely to occur. Flexible and close communications with children's families ensure that staff members are made aware if there are any problems outside of school that might be having an impact on a particular child's wellbeing, and this can also be recorded in each child's individual profile.

Where tracking shows that an individual child is causing concern, parents are contacted, and the inclusion team steps up their support for the child. A written plan may be made in conjunction with the child and their parents, showing clear targets for improvement and monitoring. The focus of these plans is not only in identifying the improvements that need to be made, but also in detailing the support that will be put in place in order to enable the child to succeed.

The school's policy on rewards also takes a trauma-informed approach. The policy states that, 'We create an ethos of every child as an individual...and achievement is based on their own personal progress – not as a comparison with others.' Children's achievements are acknowledged by positive feedback, sharing their work, stickers (not counted or displayed on a chart), communications home and achievement assemblies held each week. Each day, one child in every class is chosen to be the VIP for the day. Other children and the staff give positive comments about this child, which are recorded on a scroll and sent home with them. The head teacher and the governors are also involved in recognising hard work, kindness and contributions to school life. None of these rewards are competitive, and none are recorded on public charts which could be used to compare the skills, abilities or achievements of a particular individual or group. The emphasis is on making progress at an individual level – doing better today than you did yesterday.

Colebourne is an orderly and calm environment. Routines and consistent approaches are the bedrock to maintaining this atmosphere, and the school embraces a 'high structure, high nurture' philosophy, emphasising time in over time out, natural consequences, and using staff presence to help children to regulate. The school's latest Ofsted report describes leadership and management, and behaviour and safety of pupils as 'outstanding' and says, 'Pupils behave exceptionally well in lessons and at all other times during the school day. They show impeccable manners towards each other and to adults. This makes the school a very safe place in which pupils can learn.'

Chapter 7

TRANSITIONS

In this chapter:

Transitions from home to school and school refusal

Transitions from one activity to another

Transitions from school terms to holidays and back again

Transitions to a new class or school

From the moment a student arrives at the school gates, school life is a series of transitions to be navigated. Even in the course of an ordinary school day, children will transition several times from one area or room to another, from one activity to another, and one teacher to another. Arriving at school at the start of the day, and leaving at the end are also significant daily transition times, and at the end of most school years, there will be transition to a new classroom, timetable or even school, with new teachers and routines to learn, and a new environment to get used to.

Transitions from home to school and school refusal

It is quite normal for very young children to find transitions at the start and end of the pre-school or nursery day difficult, but for some children, these difficulties can persist even into the secondary school years. A child may signal obvious distress by crying, screaming and even becoming violent at home before school, on the way to school, or at the point of entering the building or classroom. For other children, the signs may be less obviously linked to the transition. They may employ delaying tactics while getting ready for school, going into class or starting the day's activities. They may hide or run away, complain frequently of headaches or stomach aches, withdraw and become unresponsive, or be persistently late or absent.

School refusal and problems at the school gate can be an enormous source of stress and conflict between families and schools. Parents may feel as though there must be a problem in school if their child is so reluctant to go there, while schools may suspect that parents are not being firm enough, or are not encouraging positive attitudes towards education. Attendance is a measurable factor, and there is pressure on both schools and families to ensure that children attend school regularly, with lavish prizes being awarded for 100 per cent attendance in some schools.

In considering what lies behind school refusal and anxiety, it is helpful to avoid the temptation to assign blame to any party. The child's behaviour is communicating a need, and that need may not be rooted in the most obvious place. Many children who have experienced trauma, abuse and neglect will also have experienced several dramatic and often sudden transitions in their early lives. They may have been removed from birth families, and lived with relatives or foster carers before settling into their permanent home. These transitions are sometimes abrupt, and always devastating. They erode a child's trust and ability to form positive attachments even if the child does not consciously remember them. For a child who is not secure in the knowledge that their caregiver will be there at the end of the day, transitions into school can trigger deep feelings of loss or fear of abandonment.

While separation anxiety is a normal developmental stage in a young child's development, in some cases, it can persist long beyond the toddler years, even into adulthood. School-aged children with separation anxiety may experience physical symptoms such as headaches, nausea and vomiting in anticipation of a separation from their attachment figure and, once separated, may become withdrawn and distracted. The impact of separation anxiety on an older child is not limited to the periods of time immediately around a separation. It may also manifest as a persistent fear of being alone and ongoing anxiety about the possibility of a separation caused by an unexpected event (for example, an illness or death).

Any transition involves change. A child who feels unsafe may resist change and fight to retain control of their situation. Even though they may have been through the same transition many times before, if they are in a heightened state of anxiety it may be hard for them to think logically about what is coming at the other side of the transition, so they become intent on maintaining the current situation. This anxiety-fuelled need to control can explain why some children struggle with the transition home at the end of the day.

There may also be environmental triggers. The start and end of the school day can be noisy, crowded and sometimes rushed. Children with sensory issues have a lot to process at times when a class full of children are all putting their coats and belongings in a crowded cloakroom, or hundreds of students are filling narrow corridors in a headlong rush for the exits. If the morning routine prior to coming to school, or the final lesson of the day, were rushed or difficult, anxiety may be raised in advance of the transition, making any sensory issues even more apparent.

While problems at the school gate are not necessarily indicators that there is a problem in school, this possibility should also be considered. Clearly if a child is experiencing distress at school, and perceives that school is not a safe place, this will have an impact on their ability to smoothly transition at the start of the school day.

> Our school has been fantastic. I'm able to ring ahead and let them know he's having a difficult morning; they'll have a teaching assistant (TA) ready to take charge as we approach. They allow him to go to Breakfast Club for free...to avoid separation anxiety in the playground.

Approaches to try

- Allow the parent or carer to bring the child in at a different entrance and at a slightly earlier or later time to reduce sensory overload and promote as calm a handover as possible.

- Arrange for the key adult (see Chapter 3) to meet and greet the child at the start of the day and say goodbye at the end of the day, signifying that the child or young person is moving from one safe base to another.

- Direct the child or young person towards a structured activity immediately on their arrival at school, rather than allowing them to wait, loosely supervised, in the school grounds until the day formally begins. This could involve carrying out a specific task in the library or sports department (according to the child's interest), arranging chairs in the classroom, or structured time with the key adult.

- Allow the child to bring in a transition object from home. This could be a small soft toy, an object belonging to a parent or carer, a spray of perfume or aftershave on a hanky, a passport photograph of their parent or carer, or similar.

- Be very clear with the child about what will happen after the transition. Regular routines at the start and end of the school day can support this, although a child experiencing anxiety may need these explicitly described to them in the moment even if they have experienced the routines many times.

- Maintain open communications with parents and carers around any difficulties the child may have experienced in the morning before coming to school, and also around any concerns about school that the child may have expressed at home.

- React to the child's developmental age, rather than their chronological age. Acknowledge their negative feelings around the transition, and avoid phrases such as, 'You're such a big girl now, you should be fine with leaving your mummy', or, 'Look! None of the other children are crying.'

- End the day on a positive note. Even if there have been negative incidents during the day, do not discuss these with the parent or carer in front of the child at pick-up time.

Transitions from one activity to another

Anybody who has had to negotiate a reluctant child away from the park at the end of the day will know that children can sometimes have difficulty transitioning from one activity to another, especially if they are particularly enjoying, or particularly engrossed in, what they are doing. For children who have experienced trauma and attachment difficulties, struggles with these types of transition can continue well beyond their early years.

A strong desire to control the environment is one way in which traumatised children can establish a feeling of safety. Naish (2018, p.193) explains it like this: 'Control is a fear-based behaviour and their behaviour is saying, "I can't trust adults to be in charge yet." In a classroom, the adults are, very necessarily, in charge. Routines and boundaries are set by adults and apply to all, and, although children who have experienced trauma and attachment difficulties desperately need these boundaries to be in place in order to reinforce their sense of safety, they may also resist the perceived loss of control that comes with them. Their response can be to internalise their distress – for example, to blankly ignore the teacher's instruction to finish the activity in apparent defiance – or to externalise it by, for instance, shouting, verbally refusing, becoming angry or crying.

These behaviours are not rooted in defiance, but in fear. The child may be unwilling to relinquish control to another person, even an adult, because they do not fully trust that adult. They may be unable to see beyond the task they are engaged in to look forward to the new activity they are supposed to transition to. Fear may be mixed with frustration or even panic if a child feels under pressure to complete their current task in a rush because a transition is imminent. For children with a poor sense of the abstract concept of time, transitions may seem to come upon them without warning, and fear of punishment for unfinished work, or a self-imposed perfectionism, can result in negative reactions to the thought of moving from one activity to another.

Approaches to try

- Difficulty with transitions from one activity to another are not restricted only to children who have experienced trauma; often strategies that support children with autistic spectrum disorder with transitions will be of benefit to other children too.

- Visual timetables can be helpful in ensuring children have a clearer understanding of what will happen throughout the day. For children moving from classroom to classroom, these need to be portable.

- Strong, predictable routines around transitions are important; difficulties are more likely to arise if transitions are rushed and seem to arrive from nowhere.

- Provide a specific location for the child to put items or work they have finished with at the end of the activity, and another box for things that can be finished later. This establishes a repeated routine to the end of each activity and reduces anxiety over unfinished tasks.

- Give advance warning of upcoming transitions; some children may benefit from a visual timer to help them plan, but others may find that puts too much pressure on them to complete the task and sends them into panic.

- Consider using strategies to warn about an upcoming transition, other than the teacher announcing it; for example, place a sign up on the board, or play a musical chime.

- If children are engaged in a timed task, for example, if a certain amount of work needs to be completed before the next transition, ensure that they are well supported to plan their time. Children with executive functioning difficulties will find this a struggle, and may well be caught out as transition time approaches, leading to heightened anxiety, or causing them to give up altogether.

- If difficulties arise when moving from an activity a child really likes, to one that they don't enjoy as much, consider inserting a short, neutral activity in between.

- Where transition occurs after a long period of quiet or stillness, or after intense activity, children may benefit from sensory activity to support them through the transition and re-set their state for the next activity, for example, carrying a pile of books to the shelf, moving some heavy furniture, eating a chewy or crunchy snack or listening to some calming music.

Transitions from school terms to holidays and back again

The end of term is often a welcome transition for many students and teachers, but it can be just another difficult time of year for others. As the holidays approach, and especially the summer holidays, many schools begin to wind down, timetables become more flexible, and populated with trips, school concert or show rehearsals, special assemblies and sports days. These activities are designed to be fun, and are often a vital part of school life and community, but for children who need predictability, structure and routine in order to feel calm and safe, they can raise anxiety and lead to an increase in unwanted behaviours. We will look in more detail about how to handle variety and change in Chapter 9, but for now it is enough to know that these events and treats can exacerbate transition anxieties at the end of term.

Similarly, the return to the structured, timetabled environment of school after a period of less structured holiday time, can also require significant adjustments on the part of the child. After a longer holiday, routines, strategies and even hard-won learning can be forgotten, meaning that a child may appear to have regressed considerably on their return to the classroom and extra support will be needed during the settling-in period.

School holidays tend to move with the rhythm of the seasons. The new school year heralds the coming of autumn; the early part of the spring term may be marked by cold and snow or driving rain; the latter half of the summer term is accompanied by warmer temperatures and sunshine. Children who have experienced traumatic events may have sensory and conscious memories of those events which are tied up with the seasons and the weather. For instance, a child may remember being led away from their birth family's house for the last time down a snow-covered path, or have deep memories of a distressing final contact with birth parents as the summer sun illuminated the institutional surroundings of a local authority contact centre. If a child seems to have difficulty with a certain time of year, major school transitions that coincide with that will only exacerbate the situation.

Approaches to try

- Maintain open communication with parents and carers to ensure everybody is aware of times of year that might be especially difficult for the child because of past trauma.

- Keep the routines and structures of the classroom and school as near to normal as possible throughout the final weeks of term.

- When 'wind down' activities are planned, ensure that children who struggle with this have a selection of alternative structured activities available to them.

- See Chapter 9 for more ideas on how to manage theme days, special events and holidays.

- As far as possible, retain the same staff members from one term to another so that when the children return from the holidays, they are greeted by the same, familiar faces.

- Warn children in advance if any major changes to the school building, outside areas or classroom are planned during the holiday period.

- Allow the child to take home a transitional object from school for the holidays, for example the class teddy bear or pet, a plant from the classroom, a book from the library. This reassures them that they will be coming back.

- Acknowledge the difficulty that big transitions can bring and assure the child that you are aware of their big feelings and are there to support them.

- Key adults should try to maintain some indirect contact during the holiday period where possible. Even a short postcard saying that you are looking forward to seeing the child again at the start of the new term can reassure the child that they are held in mind and their safe base is still there for them.

- Be prepared for some regression at the start of the new term. A child may re-visit separation anxiety behaviours that were thought to be long overcome, for instance, and extra support may be required for the first days or weeks.

Transitions to a new class or school

Change of class or school means loss, and can bring up mixed feelings for children as they approach the end of the school year. Even if the key adult is to remain the same, the likelihood is that there will be new teachers, new support staff and sometimes new classmates. Children who may already have lost their birth families, their foster carers and much more in their short lives are particularly vulnerable to the loss of the relationships they have developed with the teachers and other adults they have known. Each of these losses may be processed as a very personal rejection, and the child may learn to protect themselves by rejecting before they are rejected, leading to an increase in unwanted behaviours directed at members of staff, particularly those the child has been closest to. It is important to remember that, however it seems, this is not personal and comes from a place of deep-rooted fear and hurt within the child.

All of this is often mixed with apprehension about what the new class or school will be like, and fear of the unknown. As we have discussed, loss of control, inability to imagine what the future holds and fear are all factors in making transitions difficult for children who have experienced trauma, and the scale of a transition to a new class or school only magnifies all of these concerns. Many parents and carers of children who struggle with change have found that waiting until the last minute to tell the child about the impending change can reduce unwanted behaviours. However, there is no chance of employing this strategy with the end of the school year, as everybody will know it is coming weeks in advance. The storm must simply be ridden out.

The transition from primary school to secondary school can be particularly fraught. We considered how best to support a child to settle into a new class or school separately in Chapter 5, but there is plenty that can be done in terms of preparing for the transition to a new school, while the child is still in the familiar environment of their old one. Bear in mind that not all children will have the same feelings about transitioning to secondary school. Their expectations may depend on the experiences they have had at primary school. Some children may be consumed by fear and worry, whereas others may be looking forward to a fresh start and new opportunities. Regardless, all children who have experienced trauma, attachment problems and their associated difficulties, will benefit from thorough preparation for the transition.

My child is lucky to be in a primary school which is committed to attachment training and with teachers who understand his needs. My biggest fear is that all the high schools in the area are a completely different environment. Simple things like the sheer size of them and the number of students is an overwhelming thought. I cannot envisage him coping nearly as well when he has to transition.

Approaches to try

Transition to a new class or year group:

- As far as possible, ensure that support staff will stay the same in the new year in order to provide consistency of expectations and support, and maintain relationships with the child's parents or carers; this is especially important for the key adult.

- Ensure that new teachers are thoroughly informed about the child's needs and support plans and involved early in planning meetings and reviews.

- Be prepared for an escalation in unwanted behaviours, some of which may feel personally directed, and seek support from senior leaders, inclusion, special needs and pastoral staff if necessary, both for yourself and for the child.

- Arrange whole-class and individual visits to the new classroom, or any new facilities that will feature in next year's timetable (such as science labs or technology rooms).

- Ensure the child has their new timetable as far in advance as possible, and use it to plan their week and the equipment they will need.

- Physically walk the child around the new routes they will be using in school (for example, from classroom to dining room, or from one classroom to another).

- Arrange for the new class teacher, or new head of year to have indirect contact with the child and their family during the summer holidays, for example sending postcard saying that they are looking forward to seeing the child in school in the new year.

- Prepare a short 'year in review' book, containing photos and highlights from the child's year in your class or year group. If each class teacher does this in primary school, it can form a growing document that the child can take with them from class to class, to new schools and into their adulthood.

Transition to a new school:

- Encourage parents and carers to visit the new school's open evenings as early as possible. Many secondary schools arrange open evenings for children in Year 5, which can help families to begin to introduce the subject of the changes that will be coming, long before they are imminent.

- Ensure that children who are likely to have particular difficulty with the transition have additional transition visits to their chosen secondary school. If a child is transferring mid-year, or not at the end of primary school, allow the child time off for extra transition days.

- Support parents to identify key members of staff, especially special educational needs and additional learning needs co-ordinators, inclusion officers, the designated teacher for looked-after and previously looked-after children and virtual school head,[1] head of year, etc. and ensure key information is shared with them.

---

1   A local authority appointee (in England) responsible for overseeing the education of looked-after and previously looked-after children.

- Arrange for ex-pupils who have transitioned to secondary school to visit the class and talk to all the children about their experiences.

- Use social stories as a way to talk openly about fears and anxieties.

BURY CHURCH OF ENGLAND HIGH SCHOOL
Towards effective transition support

As a state secondary school with a good local reputation, Bury Church of England High School accepts children from up to 60 primary schools, spread over a wide geographical area, making managing transitions to Year 7 a particular challenge.

The school has a long-established policy of visiting every single feeder primary school each year and meeting with Year 6 class teachers and prospective students, as well as providing extra taster days for children with identified special educational needs. More recently, the school has developed an enhanced transition programme which also supports other vulnerable children.

Information gathering begins long before applicants are due to start at the school, with a staff team incorporating senior leadership, the Department for Learning Support, and members of the pastoral team working together to identify children who may need additional support. Children who have identified special educational needs, who are looked-after or previously looked-after, who are the only student transferring from their primary school, or who are identified by their primary school teachers as likely to benefit from extra transition support, are invited to participate. Each year, this extra transition support is offered to up to 30 children out of an intake of 162, and around half of these will access the full, enhanced plan.

All children are invited to two transition days at the school, but for children on the enhanced programme, there are several additional opportunities to get to know the school, key members of staff, and other children in their cohort before the main visit days in July. As early as April or May, identified children and their families are invited to tour the school, either individually, or in small groups. Several of these tours are arranged, and children participate in as many as needed until they feel at ease in the school environment and know their way around.

Once all children who are accessing the enhanced plan have participated in the tours, a social event with a picnic is organised for them as a relationship-building opportunity between children and staff, and between children and their future classmates. They will be introduced to the Head of Year 7, the pastoral team, the Head of Lower School and the special educational needs team. The Head of Year 7 is permanently in that post and does not change from year to year, in recognition that the needs of children first arriving from primary school are distinct, and require the expertise that comes with experience.

Transition days are also an opportunity for newly arriving students to meet their peer mentors. These Year 10 students are selected while they are in Year 9, and undergo a training programme to help them recognise the difficulties that children might have on arriving in Year 7 and provide support in conjunction with staff. These older children take on a leadership role. Two are assigned to each Year 7 form group. They are available during form time and also in the playground, in recognition that some younger children find it easier to talk to their peers than to adults.

Tina Astley (Deputy Head, Care, Support and Guidance) recalls that a stint as Head of Year 7 was the catalyst for re-thinking the transition programme. 'I realised that it's a different world in Year 7. The children are still very much like primary school children, and I started thinking about what I would like for my own children, who were in primary school at the time.' Tina found that a considerable amount of her time was taken up responding to phone calls and emails from parents with concerns and questions, which was difficult to manage on top of a teaching workload. 'It wasn't that their questions were unreasonable, but it alerted me to the fact that more support and guidance was needed.'

Including parents, guardians and carers is a key part of the transition programme, ensuring that they feel involved and informed from the start. Parents are now invited to the first Year 7 assembly, carrying on a practice that is familiar to most from primary school, and a new pastoral parents' evening has been introduced after the first six weeks of the autumn term. This allows parents and carers to sit down with their children's form tutors and discuss how well they are settling in. The outcome is that parents have fewer questions, and feel more able to save any concerns they do have until the parents' evening, resulting in a dramatic drop in the number of queries to staff members during the first weeks of the autumn term. Now, all staff have more time to respond quickly to serious and urgent problems.

For the children, the introduction to a busy secondary school timetable is gradual. For the first three weeks, the children are taught entirely in their form groups, imitating the stable primary school system that they are used to. They will remain with these form tutors for their whole time at the school, and the placing of vulnerable children into their form groups is carefully managed, based on which tutors the staff team believe will be a good fit for each child. Packtype® activities [psychometric games designed to help children identify their own and others' strengths and weaknesses] for all children during the main transition days in July support this process.

The end of the first three weeks is marked by two activity days for all of Year 7. The school used to run a three-day residential, but it was felt that this was a financial burden on families, following hard on the heels of Year 6 residentials and the expense of buying new uniform. Instead, children now spend the first day at the Lowry Theatre in Manchester, exploring Lowry's art through drama activities and workshops with a visiting artist. On the second day, they visit Challenge 4 Change [an indoor activity centre based near Manchester, England] for a physical indoor activity day, working in teams. Throughout the two days, children from different form groups are gradually integrated with each other, over lunch, and shared activities. The following week, children begin timetabled lessons in their teaching groups, fresh from a shared experience, and with memories to talk about.

Just before Christmas, there is another trip for Year 7 students, and this time, parents, guardians and carers are invited. Tina explains, 'We very much see our school as a family, and this is a great opportunity to welcome parents and carers to mark the end of their child's first term, build relationships, and enjoy a fun, family day out.'

The enhanced transition programme at Bury Church of England High School is a team effort, with top-down support and leadership from the head teacher, input from the Department for Learning Support, and the pastoral team, both of which come under Tina's line management, as well as form tutors, the Head of Year 7 and the Head of Lower School. It has evolved over several years and is still evolving. It takes considerable commitment from staff members, but relies mostly on low-cost interventions based on knowledge of individual children, and the expertise of the staff. As Tina says, 'We believe that if you get it right at the beginning, you reap the benefits at the end.'

Chapter 8

TRICKY CURRICULUM

In this chapter:

Curriculum hotspots

Reading material and films

Mothers' Day and Fathers' Day

When we visit the cinema or buy a DVD or video game, there is usually a classification that indicates what age-range it is suitable for based on its content. Occasionally, a TV continuity announcer will warn us that an upcoming broadcast may contain scenes of an upsetting nature. Even music tracks are sometimes accompanied by a warning about explicit content. These warnings are designed to assist us in making choices about what is suitable material for ourselves and our children.

There are times when it would be helpful if aspects of the school curriculum came with a similar warning. Basic staples of the curriculum at all ages can pose genuine difficulties for children who have experienced trauma, and especially for those who are care-experienced, adopted or previously looked-after. While it is not always possible, or even desirable, to remove these topics altogether, awareness of their impacts and extra thought given to their planning and delivery may help to prevent children from responding negatively to material that unexpectedly triggers strong feelings.

Curriculum hotspots

Bring in a photograph of yourself as a baby. Draw a family tree. Create a timeline of key events in your life so far. If we look at any of these common tasks with a care-experienced child or young person in our mind, we can immediately see the difficulties. Children who no longer live with their birth families may not have access to family photographs. A family tree is not a simple diagram for an adopted child. While their classmates are writing, 'Age 7: I got my first pet' on their life chronologies, would a child feel comfortable writing, 'Age 3: My dad went to prison', or 'Age 4: I was taken into care'?

Tricky curriculum areas fall broadly into two categories: topics or activities that directly impact on or exclude children who have experienced trauma, are looked-after or are previously looked-after, and topics or activities that may serve as triggers to individual children depending on their circumstances.

The examples above fall into the first category. We could also include writing autobiographical stories, mapping eye colour or other characteristics in your family as part of studying genetics, researching family history, and any other topic or activity which assumes that immediate families are only biological relatives, and children remain in the same family throughout childhood.

The difficulty created by these types of activities is not only practical. In most cases, there is likely to be an alternative option for the individual, such as bringing in a random baby photo found on the internet. However, both the activity itself, and the practical workarounds proposed, create conflict for children whose backgrounds are not straightforward.

Let's take the example of the baby photo. Straightaway, the request for a baby photo that an adopted child may not have access to highlights their adoptive status, their difference. The child or their parents then have to make a decision about how to handle the request. Explaining the predicament to the teacher involves revealing personal information. While most adopted children should be aware of their own status, they may still not wish their teachers and peers to know about it. Teachers would most likely be understanding of the situation and willing to accept alternatives, but the alternatives themselves only serve to further highlight the child's different status. If the child brings in a stock baby photo, will a pretence be kept up that this is really the child's baby picture? Or will everybody need to know the truth, and the reasons for that decision?

For some children, the impulse will be to hide sensitive information about themselves and their families. If their home life is chaotic or they have experienced traumatic events within the family recently or in the past, they may feel a sense of responsibility for not revealing the reality of their home lives and situations. A child may omit to mention on their personal timeline that a parent was incarcerated for instance, while internally being thrown into a state of turmoil over the reminder of that event.

Other children may be prompted by such activities to share very personal information. This may be in the form of a disclosure, or simply a case of a child naively over-sharing details about themselves and their lives which they may later come to regret, for instance, revealing their adoptive or looked-after status to the whole class while giving a talk on 'My Life'. Once spoken, the words can never be taken back.

While some topics or activities are likely to cause difficulties for any child who has experienced trauma, or is care-experienced, others may serve as triggers only for individual children depending on their particular circumstances. These may be linked to specific occurrences or incidents in a child's life, or may be more generalised, relating to themes of loss, rejection, abandonment or fear, for instance.

> In Year 4 they worked on World War II evacuees who eventually returned to their parents. This created three months of additional anxiety. It never crossed the school's mind, the mental anguish it caused.

As part of foster care training, potential carers are introduced to the concept of being a behaviour detective. It is not possible to know everything about a child that comes into a foster carer's home, so all triggers cannot be avoided, but depending on what a child has experienced, even certain sounds and smells can be triggers. Foster carers need to become adept at recognising anxiety and fear-fuelled behaviours arising from such triggers, and responding to the cause rather than the presenting behaviour. Carers are trained to re-arrange their households to minimise potential triggers, including, for instance, avoiding spending time in a fostered child's bedroom, or leaving the door open if they do. Similarly, teachers cannot know the intimate life history of every child in their classroom, but can be aware that some unexpected and unwanted reactions can occur as a result of triggers related to a child's traumatic experiences.

As children move through their school years, more and more challenging topics are introduced. Themes such as sex and relationships, drug and alcohol abuse, bullying, and crime and punishment may have direct links to experiences that some children have faced. Children who have experienced trauma may have a stronger reaction than others to topics referencing sensitive content, such as issues relating to war, terrorism, bereavement, or the plight of refugees, even if it is not directly connected to their experience. The themes covered in special assemblies by organisations like the NSPCC or Barnardo's might be too close to home for some. A child who has been taken into care may see aspects of their own experience reflected in children who were evacuated during World War II. Asking those children to, for instance, write a diary entry from the point of view of an evacuated child risks awakening all the trauma and grief of their own experience.

These individual triggers are particularly difficult for a class teacher to navigate. The range of potential triggers, and the range of possible responses to these, makes it very difficult for all eventual possibilities to be predicted. Some children will not make the link between the subject matter and their own experience, and sail through the topic oblivious. Others may seem fine in the classroom, but react once they are home. However, if a child is experiencing an unexplained increase in anxiety-fuelled behaviour, then triggers in the current curriculum are always worth considering as a possible cause.

Approaches to try

- Look at your curriculum with a 'trauma lens' and make a note of activities and topics which may be upsetting or triggering. Consider current trauma as well as historical experiences. The simple request, 'Tell me what you did during the holidays' can be terribly humiliating for a child who lives in a chaotic home, or who may have spent the whole time caring for a parent or younger siblings and has no lovely stories of holidays or day trips to tell.

- Speak to parents and carers of looked-after, adopted and previously looked-after children about their child's particular needs. Some children will have triggers which are well known to their families.

- Avoid making changes to topics and activities that only apply to children who are adopted, looked-after, or particularly vulnerable for another reason, as being singled out adds to their feeling of difference and highlights it.

- Consider the learning objective of activities which may be problematic, and find ways to deliver the same objective in a different way for the whole class. For example: explore themes of growing up, change and chronology using photographs of yourself over time, rather than asking children to bring in photographs; create a family tree or timeline of a famous or historical figure; use non-human or hypothetical examples to investigate genetics.

- Ensure that all parents and carers are aware of the topics their child's class will be covering each term. It is not possible to avoid all difficult topics, and neither is it possible to shield children forever, but involved parents and carers can prepare their children for topics that might evoke big feelings, and work with the school to find strategies to support the child. This is better for everybody than managing a crisis after it has erupted.

- Make sure parents and carers are aware of visitors to the school, and special events which may highlight sensitive subject matter.

- At times when sensitive subject matter is unavoidable, ensure that there is a safe place for affected children to go, preferably with key adults available.

- Be aware that children who have experienced trauma may react more strongly than others to upsetting news stories, and that discussions of those stories in class and around the school may provoke anxiety-fuelled behaviours.

- Resist the urge to compare children. Every human being processes adverse experiences in their own way. Just because the last adopted child you taught was fine with this topic, it does not mean the next one will be.

Reading material and films

Stories and films where children are the protagonists seem to rely heavily on plot devices that remove the children's parents in the first few scenes, or even before the story has begun. The world of children's literature and film is replete with orphans. Think of Harry Potter, Anne of Green Gables, Lyra from *His Dark Materials*, Peter Pan, Sophie from *The BFG*, and even the three children in *Despicable Me*.

Sometimes, the child's orphanhood is an essential part of their story but, in many cases, perfectly acceptable parents are unceremoniously dispatched purely so that the child heroes can go about their exploits unhindered by inconveniences such as regular bedtimes or healthy meals. Bereavement or abandonment is little more than a plot device, and cruel step-parents and guardians regularly mete out arbitrary punishments in order to set up a scenario whereby children will be rescued by a fantasy benefactor, or will somehow save themselves.

The orphaned child with a wicked guardian is such a common trope in children's literature that we often don't pause to think about it. It is even possible that children whose own experiences directly resonate with the characters in the books they are reading don't notice the connection because they have become so used to it. Recognising the ubiquitous nature of the theme of the abandoned and orphaned child is, however, a wake-up call to adults that books, films, art and music are just as likely to contain triggering themes and content as the most sensitive parts of our school curriculum.

Think about the stories that you plan to read to your class, or that you will expect them to read, the films you might show them as an end of term treat, or the books in the class reading corner or school library. Many will directly reference children who have lost their parents, who have been caught up in war or tragedy, who have been bullied, or attacked or abused in some way. While some children may be able to separate these fictional experiences from their own without even thinking about it, others, and especially children whose developmental and emotional age is younger than their chronological age, might find such material more difficult to cope with. A mild on-screen thrill can evoke genuine terror in some, and something that is 'Just a story!' to most children might be a horribly accurate portrayal of remembered experiences to others. Older children who are 'young for their age' may struggle to separate fiction from reality, and become anxious about things they have read in stories, even to the point of experiencing nightmares. Others may adopt the fantasies presented to them in fiction as being more palatable than the reality, holding on to them fiercely just as little orphan Annie held on to her broken locket.

We can't shield children from difficult topics in the curriculum for ever and neither can we weed out every story, book, song or film that might upset them. Trauma-informed practice is not concerned with trapping children in their difficulties through removing all expectations, but in recognising the challenges they face, and supporting them to make progress from where they are, not where we wish they were. It is hoped that every person who has experienced trauma will one day be able to come out from under its shadow, but that will not happen by magic. If a child feels safe at school, and has good attachment relationships with key adults, then, supported by their parents or carers, they may benefit from the exploration of challenging themes through fiction, film, song and drama. This is not the same as expecting them to 'get on with it' or 'toughen up', or manage their strong feelings unsupported.

It undoubtedly takes up valuable time checking books, films and other resources for potentially triggering content, but this time is likely to be amply re-paid in the form of a quieter, calmer classroom if doing so helps to avoid raising the anxiety levels of particularly vulnerable children.

Approaches to try

- Review the books, stories, films and other material you plan to share with your class with a trauma-lens, making yourself aware of any challenging themes.

- Ensure that all parents and carers have a complete list of such materials in advance so that they can familiarise themselves with the content and support and prepare their child.

- Plan to have support in place when difficult themes will be covered, including access to key adults and availability of a safe space.

- If children have free choice of class or library books, discuss with parents and carers how best to support children to choose books that will be suitable, without singling them out. Where possible, involve children in this process with the aim of enabling them to make informed choices.

- Where resources do contain challenging material, acknowledge this, and offer support. Avoid issuing a blanket 'trigger warning' as this puts the responsibility on the child to take action to protect themselves, whereas children need adults to support them to manage big feelings.

- Be aware that a child may be unsettled by material without knowing why. If there is a rise in anxiety-fuelled behaviours (including avoidance and dissociation), consider the possibility that issues raised by stories, books and films may lie beneath it.

* * *

Listening to a story, reading quietly, or watching a documentary or film in class can be difficult for some children, even if there is no challenging content involved, as it requires children to sit still, to sit quietly and to pay attention, sometimes for long periods. Children who have experienced early trauma may find this particularly difficult, even if they are older, for a number of reasons:

- Poor core strength may mean that a child finds it physically tiring to sit still on a chair, or on the floor unsupported for long periods.

- A child who is hypo-sensitive to vestibular and proprioceptive input (see Chapter 2) may wriggle and fidget to get the sensory input they need while sitting still.

- Hyper-vigilant children may find themselves distracted by unexplained noises around them in a quiet classroom, or by movements they see out of the corner of their eye.

- Unexpected loud noises in films and videos may startle those with auditory sensory processing difficulties.

- Films and videos can contain a lot of visual stimulation that may impact on children with visual sensory processing difficulties, especially if the room has been darkened.

- Many children with Foetal Alcohol Spectrum Disorder (FASD) have attention difficulties, finding it difficult to settle down and to filter out distractions and concentrate consistently.

- Children with poor receptive language skills may struggle to follow a story being read aloud, lose interest, and begin to fidget and disrupt out of boredom.

- Similarly, children whose reading skills lag behind their peers will have to work much harder at silent reading, tiring more quickly.

- Reading aloud in class is particularly challenging for children who lack confidence, who fear being ridiculed or who value the safety that they find in being effectively invisible. In those circumstances, a child may even prefer to be excluded from the lesson than participate in an activity that causes them deep anxiety.

Approaches to try

- Provide a sensory break before and after to give children the vestibular and proprioceptive input they need. Activities such as carrying stacks of books, or pushing furniture out of the way, can be incorporated into the preparation for the quiet period.

- Ensure children are sitting comfortably and are well-supported, with back support if on the floor.

- Use wobble cushions and wedge cushions for 'active sitting' for restless, fidgety children, to improve seated posture and increase proprioceptive input.

- Allow hyper-vigilant, easily distracted children to sit against the wall at the side or the back of the room so they have a clear view of the classroom, making them less likely to turn around in their seats in response to movements and noises.

- Allow the use of ear defenders for children who react strongly to auditory input.

- Read aloud in short chunks, pausing regularly to re-focus children and ensure they are following.

- Try paired reading aloud with a partner instead of reading aloud to the class or reading in silence.

- Actively teach, reinforce and model good listening skills regularly.

Mothers' Day and Fathers' Day

While Mothers' and Fathers' Days are not the only celebratory days that weave themselves into the school curriculum, they can be particularly challenging celebrations for children who are adopted, looked-after, previously looked-after or experiencing other kinds of family difficulty and, as such, they deserve some special attention.

Perhaps in recognition of the complexity of modern families, Fathers' Day is often less celebrated, and less ubiquitous in the media than Mothers' Day. Schools have become used to encouraging children to create cards and gifts for a variety of male role models, recognising that there will be those in every classroom who do not live with, or even have contact with, their birth fathers. In some schools, Fathers' Day passes without celebration.

Mothers' Day, however, is still widely recognised, and its approach is heralded by an intense period of advertising, idealising the mother–child relationship. Both approaches can cause difficulties for children from non-standard family backgrounds.

Since 2006, there have been nearly 3000 adoptions recorded for same-sex families in the UK. In the year ending March 2017, 10 per cent of adoptions were to single adopters, and just under 10 per cent were to same-sex couples in England alone. At any given time, there are approximately 95,000 children in the care of local authorities across the UK, who may be living with foster carers or relatives, in children's homes or elsewhere. Add to this the tens of thousands of children who are permanently placed with relatives or others on different legal orders, and it is clear that traditional approaches to Mothers' and Fathers' Days could be problematic for huge numbers of children who, for whatever reason, can no longer live with their birth parents.

> When my four-year-old adopted son brought home the invitation to the 'Mothers Day Tea Party', I phoned the school to ask if I, as one of two dads, would be able to attend. At first they suggested he bring in a female relative. It took several phone calls before it was agreed that my son would be allowed to bring his parent to this event, like the other children.

While some care-experienced children's difficulties around celebrating Mothers' and Fathers' Days may overlap with children who have experienced family separation, parental bereavement, or who live in single or same-sex parent households, children who have been permanently removed from their birth families can also experience specific additional conflicts around the existence of a day where parents are celebrated.

Let's consider Mothers' Day from the perspective of, for example, an adopted child. This child has two mothers: their adoptive mother and their birth mother. Which mother should they celebrate? Does making a card for their adoptive mother somehow betray their birth mother? If Mothers' Day makes them think about their birth mother, does this betray their adoptive mother? A child who has memories of neglect and abuse in their birth family may struggle to reconcile those memories with the idealised notions of motherhood portrayed on Mothers' Day. An adopted child may also have conflicted feelings towards the adoptive mother who seems to have replaced their birth mother, which Mothers' Day only serves to highlight.

Even if your school makes no mention of Mothers' or Fathers' Day, has no card-making lessons, and puts on no special events, the existence of these days is impossible to ignore. While some care-experienced children will be unaffected, many will find these times of year upsetting even if their attention is not drawn to it in school, leading to an increase in anxiety and trauma-fuelled behaviours. Some may not even be able to pinpoint the source of their own distress.

Approaches to try

- Be aware that Mothers' and Fathers' Days can raise difficult feelings for many children. Increase supervision and support, especially by key adults, and involve parents and carers in plans for any celebration that will take place in school.

- Ensure that plans for celebrating these days account for the full range of diverse families represented in school, and in society as a whole. See it as an opportunity to celebrate family in all its forms.

- If the children are to make cards in class time, allow all children to make several cards for whomever they choose. Avoid singling out children and providing them with individualised alternative activities.

- Remain neutral if children choose to make cards for unexpected people, for example, birth parents they have no memory of. Resist the urge to encourage them to make a card for their carer or adoptive parent instead. Speak to the parents or carers privately about this if appropriate.

- Be careful about the language used in school and about assumptions around what a mother or a father is. Not all mothers give birth to their children, for instance. Most adoptive families avoid the terms 'real mum' or 'real dad' and instead use terms such as 'birth mum' or 'first mum'. Check with families to make sure you know the terms their children are familiar with.

Chapter 9

VARIETY AND CHANGE

Theme days, school trips and class celebrations are all designed to bring some variety into the experience of learning but, for children who rely on the security of predictable routines in order to feel safe enough to relax and learn, variety really can be the enemy. It can take years for some traumatised children to trust the adults around them and the routines that are in place to support them, so that they can stop focusing on their own survival and start focusing on learning. For children with disabilities such as Foetal Alcohol Spectrum Disorder (FASD), the need for structure, routine and scaffolding may always be there. When adults change, or routines are disrupted, even for a pleasant activity, it is all too easy for children primed for danger, and disorientated by change, to fall back on the coping mechanisms that served them so well in their early lives but which may be wholly out of place in school.

> She gets very anxious if there is a change at school, for example, school trips, if the teacher is away, if she doesn't get to eat her biscuit at the 'normal' time. Her anxiety is expressed via the medium of anger, lashing out at other children and defiance which can last the entire school day.

Theme days and special weeks

What special events are planned in your school this year? Maybe there are non-uniform days, or a special fundraising day for a national or local charity? It's likely that a varied school year will also include sports days, guest visitors, and days, or even whole weeks, themed around a particular topic, such as anti-bullying week, or science day. Events such as these are often a highlight of the school calendar, eagerly anticipated by children and staff alike.

However, any change, even a positive and fun event, can unsettle a child. Something as simple as a non-uniform day is likely to raise the excitement levels of a class full of children, if only because of the novelty value of seeing their classmates in normal clothes, or their teachers in fancy dress. For children who are less able to regulate themselves, for whatever reason, excitement and fun can be just as difficult to manage and control as anger and shame. While other children are excited, the poorly regulated child may become giddy. While other children are talking and laughing, the poorly regulated child may become overly loud and boisterous. When the other children settle down at the teacher's request, the poorly regulated child may find it much more difficult to switch off the excitement and calmly get on with their work.

We have seen in Chapters 1 and 2 how infant neglect and abuse, and even trauma that takes place prior to birth, can affect the development of a child's healthy stress response systems, and make it more difficult for them to self-regulate. While most may not view a science week or a fundraising day as a stressful experience, the change from the normal routine can throw some children into a state of stress. A child with executive functioning difficulties, for instance, who relies on a visual timetable and a well-established routine, will find these supports suddenly useless if their class is to be off timetable or using different rooms, or seeing different teachers for a theme week. Guest visitors and special activities, such as hands-on experiments, or dressing up in period clothes, may provide additional challenges for those with sensory processing difficulties. A child with attachment difficulties who relies on their key adult to be a safe base is likely to struggle if their teacher is suddenly replaced by a stranger, and their key adult is assigned to a special group activity.

When children need to make themselves feel safe by being in control of their environment, any change to that environment can make them feel out of control and unsafe. A child who feels unsafe is likely to show it through their behaviour. They may withdraw, internalising their distress, becoming extremely compliant or silent, and unresponsive to such a degree that they appear defiant, or seeking to establish safety through controlling behaviours. Some children may externalise their distress in the form of attachment-seeking behaviour (such as chattering, clinginess, separation anxiety, constant interruptions), hair-trigger anger in response to slight provocations, competitive behaviours, and other responses that can be disruptive in the classroom. Teachers may find that children experiencing this stress may seem to lose skills they had previously mastered, forget basic rules and equipment, and disregard well-established classroom codes, such as raising their hand before speaking.

Exposure to a variety of novel and interesting experiences is part of a full and rich educational experience that will benefit all children. Children who find change disorientating, and who struggle to regulate themselves through exciting or stressful experiences, will need extra support to make the most of these experiences but, if that support can be provided, inclusion in the activity will promote the child's sense of belonging to the community, and provide much needed fun and playfulness, vital to a stressed and anxious child.

Approaches to try

- Ensure that parents and carers are informed of any special events or theme days well in advance so that they can begin to prepare their child at home, and ensure that any equipment or special clothing is made ready, and is suitable for the child.

- Discuss and plan strategies for managing known special events as part of the child's regular reviews, involving key members of staff, parents and carers, and the child if appropriate.

- Try to maintain as many basic procedural routines as possible, even if the normal activities of the day are disrupted, for example, by maintaining routines around registration, meet and greet, beginning and ends of lessons, lunchtime and the end of the day.

- Ensure that the events of the day are planned in advance and can be incorporated into a visual timetable for those that need that support.

- Intersperse quieter, calm-down activities among the more active and exciting activities.

- Be prepared to allow a struggling child to access their key person, a calm-down zone, or an alternative activity.

- Note and respond to cues from an anxious child, such as foot-tapping, tense body posture, increased chattering or noise-making, fist-clenching.

- Remind all children frequently of the established code of conduct, providing examples of how children can keep to the code even though the usual routine has been altered.

- Ensure that instructions are especially clear, short and sequenced; children who are excited or stressed may not be as receptive to the teacher's voice as they would be on other days.

- If a special event means that children will be visiting unfamiliar parts of the school building, or meeting new members of staff, allow the children to see these rooms, or meet these members of staff before the event.

- When a visitor comes to the classroom, ensure that familiar members of staff stay in the classroom, especially key adults.

- Ensure that all children understand that the special event is time limited, using visual timetables to show children when normal activities will be resumed.

Christmas and other celebrations

For children who have experienced early trauma or neglect and who have been removed from their birth families, Christmas, birthdays and other celebrations need managing carefully. The excitement and expectations surrounding these special events can build to fever pitch, sometimes weeks and months in advance, leading to unexpected and unwanted reactions.

A child whose internal view of themselves is very negative can find it hard to accept gifts and attention, and may sabotage the plans for the day, or even break or destroy their new presents. If needing to control the environment is important for a child, they may become very unsettled by the plans for a celebration, the disruption to their routine and the possibility of surprises. Any special occasion that emphasises family times can cause conflict for a child who has lost their birth family. They may have memories of Christmases that went wrong in the past, or find it difficult to manage conflicting loyalties with their current parents or carers and their previous ones. As celebrations approach, parents or carers of traumatised children will often find themselves managing difficult situations at home that can then spill over into school.

Celebrations can also mean disruption to the usual school routine. How are birthdays celebrated in your classroom? Do you sing to the child whose birthday it is, or allow them to wear a special birthday hat or badge for the day? A child who relies on maintaining invisibility to secure their feeling of safety may find such a public display intolerable. Some children find it very difficult to celebrate along with others, reacting to another child's birthday celebrations with jealousy. When a child has experienced competing with their siblings for such basic survival staples as food, their drive to compete for survival can lead them to feel dangerously anxious any time another child appears to be getting something extra or special. A birthday is a reminder of a child's chronological age, but children with developmental trauma, FASD or other hidden disabilities may be functioning emotionally and socially at a younger age, and respond to special events more like a much younger child might be expected to.

It is common in schools to celebrate festivals from various cultures at different times of the year. Children are likely to have an emotional connection with festivals that are most relevant to their culture of origin, so it is important to be aware of a child's heritage when planning for celebrations in school. Some children may sail through Christmas without incident, but have a strong reaction rooted in trauma when Eid comes around.

However, Christmas, above all other celebrations, is most likely to disrupt the usual routine of school life. Many schools will provide Christmas-themed activities during class time, concerts, shows and nativity performances, fundraising and fun day events linked to the season, and decorations in classrooms and corridors. Even if little reference is made to Christmas in school, it will be ubiquitous on TV, in the media, in shops and everywhere for weeks in advance, and the timing of Christmas at the end of the autumn term means that it coincides with the run-up to a school holiday, which can be unsettling in itself, especially when children are tired at the end of a long term in school.

> The school didn't understand how it dysregulated my child at Christmas time with seven weeks of nativity rehearsals. Our family was at breaking point due to the anger from dysregulation both before and after school.

Christmas can be a challenging and tiring time for adults as well as children. It can raise uncomfortable emotions, and the stress of Christmas shopping, preparing for the day itself, and managing lots of extra activities in school can weigh on adults in school heavily. It is important for teachers and school staff to manage their own stress and emotional responses around Christmas, as well as being aware of children's responses. Other adults in children's lives may find Christmas stressful too. Some children will have experienced Christmas as a time when adults are anxious, drinking more heavily and short of money. Christmas can also be a time when family arguments and incidences of domestic violence increase.

In school, children may respond to the expectations and changes around Christmas by increasing anxious and clingy behaviours, responding more emotionally to incidents than usual, refusing to participate in activities, and sabotaging celebratory events perhaps as a way to avoid participating in them. Some children may be able to voice their feelings about Christmas, but for others, it will come out in their behaviour. When all of this is added to the difficulties around transitioning to the school holidays (see Chapter 7), the situation in school can become explosive.

Approaches to try

- Speak to the class as Christmas approaches, acknowledging that this can be a stressful time. This gives permission for children to share difficult feelings and may allow you to identify children who are likely to struggle.

- Be aware that if a child is talking incessantly about Christmas or their birthday, this may signify anxiety about the event rather than excitement.

- Provide visual timetables showing any changes to the usual routine, including rehearsals for shows, or special activities planned for the class.

- Be very clear about what will happen on celebration days, and avoid surprises.

- Plan alternative activities for children who are struggling, and allow access to calm-down zones.

- Step up support from the child's key adult.

- Plan carefully for any parties held in school. Children with a history of food scarcity may find a buffet spread with party food unbearably tempting, and disco music and loud party games can pose problems for those with sensory processing difficulties.

- Maintain procedural routines as far as possible, such as routines around the start and end of the day, lunchtime and taking the register.

- Check with individual children whether they are comfortable to participate in activities to recognise their birthday such as being sung to, or wearing a badge.

- Incorporate strategies from Chapter 7 to support children as they transition to the Christmas holidays.

School trips and holidays

The prospect of a day trip or holiday organised by school brings together all that we have already discussed around transitions, disruptions to routine and managing strong feelings of excitement and anxiety, and adds unfamiliar places, unfamiliar people, travel, and, in the case of a holiday, the prospect of sleeping away from home. Preparation is vital, although the need to adequately prepare has to be balanced against the consequences of exposing a child to weeks of mounting excitement and anxiety about what is to come.

Many of the considerations relevant to theme days in school will apply equally to day trips and holidays, and strategies to minimise disruption and anxiety will be similar both in the run-up to the trip, and during it. There will be additional concerns around safeguarding and health and safety, especially if a child is a flight risk, or is known to be unsafe around roads, for instance. Some children with attachment difficulties may indiscriminately approach strangers and will need considerable extra supervision when outside of school. Risk assessments should take account of these specific issues.

Difficulties that a child has in the classroom may be heightened and exaggerated outside of it. On a school trip, a child with sensory processing difficulties may quickly be overwhelmed by the sights and sounds of a busy museum. Children with receptive language difficulties will be trying to follow the teacher's unfamiliar instructions in a strange location, surrounded by other children whose chatter may be distracting, and without the usual routines and structures to act as a context for their understanding. Excitable children will be more excited, withdrawn children more withdrawn, and anxious children closer to the edge of their fight–flight–freeze response than usual. Sheer physical tiredness brought on by an early start, a long journey and lots of walking can contribute to children being less resilient to stress than usual.

> Ahead of their zoo trip, the children had been told that they could bring some pocket money to spend at the souvenir shop if they wished. My daughter was extremely excited about this prospect, and talked incessantly about it for days before they went. Once the children had all entered the zoo and the ticketing arrangements had been sorted out, the teacher gathered them together and explained the plan for the day to the whole group. She mentioned that they would visit the souvenir shop after lunch but, in her excitement, my daughter wasn't really listening properly and only heard 'shop'. She assumed it was time to go to the shop, and set off immediately by herself, causing a panic when her absence was noticed a few moments later.

A trip that involves an overnight stay also needs careful managing. Children who have lived in several families, have experienced being taken into foster care, or moving to live with an adoptive family, may find sleeping away from home very difficult long after their peers have become comfortable with it. Sleeping in a strange location and in a strange bed can bring back memories of unpleasant transitions, and may trigger anxiety rooted in the fear of not returning to the same home after the trip.

Despite the difficulties and the sometimes very real risks of taking traumatised children out of school for trips and holidays, it is important to make reasonable adjustments to include them wherever possible. Children with attachment difficulties, trauma histories and hidden disabilities are still entitled to the same educational opportunities as their peers, and children who feel included are more likely to co-operate with strategies to support them than children who feel excluded and unwanted. It is important that children who struggle have the opportunity to experience successes that they can build on in future. If a child feels that they cannot cope with the trip or holiday or that they are not really wanted, they may respond by refusing to go, saying that they are ill on the day, or escalating their behaviour in an attempt to be barred from participating. It is acceptable to explain to a child that they can pull out of the trip if they have to, but that the teacher wants them to be there and believes that they can succeed. This reduces the pressure on the child, while reassuring them that they are not being rejected. Knowing that their teacher or key adult believes in them and will help them to succeed can support their own self-belief and confidence.

> As well as being an adoptee, my son is non-verbal autistic and is regularly excluded from activities. The school…has even gone as far as not inviting him or informing us of school trips so that he wouldn't be there. I have no doubt that the way he is treated will have a devastating effect on his mental health now and in the future.

Approaches to try

- Ensure that parents and carers are informed about the trip or holiday well in advance, and are given a detailed itinerary so that they can prepare the child and reassure them at home. Parents or carers may wish to visit the location with their child beforehand if possible.

- Look at pictures, leaflets and websites about the location of the trip as a class, so that all children have a better idea of what to expect when they arrive.

- Ensure that key members of staff at the venue you will be visiting are aware in advance of any particular needs among the children on the trip; find out what arrangements can be made for any child who may need additional support or a calm space.

- Practise a 'trip song' or a fun 'trip game' in class during the preparation for the trip, for example, playing 'I Spy'. Incorporate this song or game at intervals on the day of the trip as a grounding and calming activity.

- When talking about the trip with the children, refer frequently to what will happen at the end of the trip, emphasising that the children will be returning home, and what will happen in school in the days following the trip, so that children are reassured that their normal routines will be restored.

- Ensure that children are under the supervision of adults they have a good prior relationship with, and who know their needs. The child's key adult is ideal.

- Use transitional objects from home for day trips and longer holidays. This could be a small toy or an item of clothing such as a scarf that belongs to their parent or carer.

- For overnight stays, allow the child to bring the pillow from their own bed. This should preferably not be freshly washed, so that it smells the same as it did the last time they slept on it.

- Have a detailed visual or written timetable of the trip that begins and ends with the child being at their home.

- Allow the child to contact home while they are on the trip. This opportunity should be discreet, but planned into the child's timetable for the day.

- Provide extra supervision for children who struggle with food issues, or who have executive functioning difficulties, to ensure that they don't eat their entire packed lunch on the coach in the morning and spend the rest of the day hungry.

- Plan unstructured time carefully, especially the end of lunchtime when some children may have finished eating long before the others; have an activity available to fill in this time in a structured way.

- In some cases, it may be appropriate for parents or carers to accompany the class on the trip. However, this is not always possible and, for some children, can create additional difficulties, so consider this on a case-by-case basis in consultation with the child's family.

- If a child is extremely anxious about the trip, or there are genuine reasons to believe the child will not cope, consider allowing the child to attend for just a part of the trip. The child's parent or carer could meet the main group partway through the day, and aim for the child to participate until the end.

- Consider how reasonable adjustments can be made for children who cannot manage a lengthy trip that is part of their required study, such as a Geography field trip. Can an alternative activity be planned, or could the whole class fulfil the requirements without an overnight stay?

Staff absence

However hard a school works to maintain consistency of staffing for vulnerable children, staff absence is sometimes unavoidable. Some absences, such as maternity leave, are known about in advance and can be planned for, but there will be days when a child arrives in the classroom, and somebody else is standing in the place of their usual teacher, or their key adult is unexpectedly away. When this happens, not only can the child be thrown into a state of anxiety by the sudden change, but the adult who is dealing with them is less likely to be aware of their specific needs and background. This is a combination which can lead to explosive consequences.

It's an old story that children will often 'play up' for the supply or substitute teacher, looking to test boundaries or explore any weaknesses, and children who have experienced trauma are not immune to this. It takes a long time for relationships to be formed between class teachers and their students, and substitute teachers do not have the luxury of this time. This may mean that unspoken classroom rules and habits are not upheld as usual, and the currency of mutual understanding between students and teachers is in short supply. The changes might be subtle, but hyper-vigilant children will quickly be aware of them, and on the alert for any shifting of the mood in the classroom. In secondary school, where children are moving from teacher to teacher, any disruption in one lesson could easily be carried over into challenging behaviour in the next.

> While the school has tried to provide a greater level of consistency for my son and made special provision, for example a time out card, the reality is that having as many as 20 professionals involved in his education has been a major cause of stress and is one of the factors that contributed to his referral to CAMHS.

When a child relies on a staff member to be their safe base in school, the sudden absence of that person can have a significant effect on the child, who may fear that the adult is gone forever, or imagine worse-case scenarios about the outcome of the adult's illness, or feel rejected or forgotten by the adult who is important to them. Attachment-based behaviours may escalate, including withdrawing and avoiding asking for help, excessive talking or noise-making, and controlling behaviours. For this reason, some schools prefer to have policies that restrict children getting too close to any one adult but, for a child with attachment difficulties, the benefits of having a key person to act as an attachment figure and safe base in school far outweigh the disadvantages, especially if strategies can be employed to minimise disruption in the event of staff absence.

Approaches to try

- In the case of a planned absence, consider allowing the child to have a transitional object from the member of staff to keep until their return. This should be something of low value, as children do lose things, but that can act as a reminder that the child will be 'held in mind' while the member of staff is away from them.

- Where possible, inform the parents or carers of vulnerable children ahead of time if a staff absence is expected, even if that means a text message before the start of a school day.

- As far as possible, replace absent staff with other adults that the children know well.

- If there is no adult known well to the class available to cover an absence, consider allowing a child who is likely to find the change difficult to spend the day in another classroom with a teacher they know well, for instance, sitting in with a class being taught by the teacher they had last year.

- Where a child has just one lesson being covered by a substitute teacher, consider allowing them to spend that lesson in an alternative location such as a pastoral room or calm-down zone.

- Ensure that replacement and substitute staff are fully appraised of vital information pertaining to children in the class, including arrangements around accessing calm-down zones and rooms.

- Step up support from the key adult if the class teacher is absent.

- Have an alternative key adult available if the child's main key adult is absent. This substitute key adult should be put in place long-term so that the child has the opportunity to form a relationship with them over time.

- If the staff absence involves a lesson where a child's usual teaching or learning support assistant is not normally present, consider altering the schedule so that the support assistant can attend that lesson on that occasion.

Chapter 10

CLASSROOM CONFRONTATIONS

In this chapter:

Angry outbursts and violence

Rudeness and arguing

Lying

The silent treatment, quiet defiance and stubborn refusals

Running and hiding

Low-level disruption, chatter and noise

Stealing and damaging property

Over-reacting, crying and whining

If you have come to this book because you are seeking strategies for a particular child whose behaviour is challenging and nothing that has been tried so far has worked, then it is likely that this is the chapter title that seems to hold most promise. So why has it been left so late in the book? Because although it may be challenging behaviour that is the most noticeable thing about a particular child, disrupting the learning of other children and draining your time and energy as a teacher, it is understanding the possible roots of persistent unwanted behaviour that will give you the best chance of actually supporting the child to move towards real change.

Being attachment- and trauma-informed is not an easy option, for the teacher, or for the child. Recognising that a child's difficulty with conforming to expectations may have its root in trauma, attachment difficulties or hidden disability is not the same as giving them a perpetual 'get out of jail free' card, any more than a diagnosis of dyslexia means that a child doesn't need to bother to learn to read at all. The more knowledge we have about why a child is struggling, the better placed we are to devise and implement strategies that will support them to make progress. Please do not lower your expectations of children who have experienced trauma. They are capable of achieving and even excelling, but the prerequisite for this success will be an approach that recognises their very real challenges, and is rooted in relationship, nurture and a commitment to inclusion.

It is part of the essential toolkit of teachers to be able to recognise problems that are limiting children's ability to make progress, and to seek out or create solutions to those problems. If you have read this far, it is likely that you have already recognised some children you know in the descriptions, and have started to think of strategies that might make a difference. In a single chapter it is not possible to cover every conceivable challenging situation that you might be faced with in the classroom, but the underpinning knowledge about trauma outlined earlier, and the examples here, will, I hope, provide you with a framework within which you can go on to use your own skills to recognise and, as far as possible within the constraints of a mass education system, meet the needs of every child that passes through your classroom.

Angry outbursts and violence

A child who frequently responds with anger, lashing out and out-of-control meltdowns not only poses a challenge for the teacher, but is also a risk to everybody around them. Shouting, screaming, growling, throwing things, hitting, kicking and biting are all actions that could see a child on a fast track to exclusion from the classroom, and eventually from the school. It is important to emphasise that the safety of everybody in the room is paramount. No adult or child comes to school expecting to be verbally or physically attacked, and frightening outbursts from one child can be the source of trauma for another.

While considering root causes of violent and dangerous behaviour, and strategies that might be put in place to prevent it and deal with the aftermath of it, we sometimes have to recognise that some children may have needs so complex that they cannot reasonably be met within the context of a mainstream school setting in a time frame that is fair for the child, and the other children in the school. However, any action to seek alternative provision for an exceptionally challenging child must be motivated by compassionate desire to achieve the best possible outcomes for that child, as well as securing the safety and protection of others. If it is necessary to remove a child from the classroom, or even from the school altogether, thought must be given as to what the child is being removed to, not only what they are being removed from. Excluding a child without a plan for suitable alternative provision where their difficulties can be properly addressed heaps additional trauma and rejection onto the child, and risks perpetuating their behaviour until their trajectory takes them onto a course that will have devastating implications for them, the people around them, and ultimately their community as a whole. Shifting a problem elsewhere is not the same as solving a problem.

A child's behaviour does not come from nowhere. It is motivated and influenced by a range of factors. While some of those factors may not be in the teacher's power to control, recognising them can enable teachers and schools to make reasonable adjustments with the aim of preventing incidents, giving the child strategies to regulate themselves, and supporting them towards reaching behaviour expectations. If a child is known to have auditory sensory processing difficulties, for instance, then it should be no surprise if they are on a hair trigger in a noisy, busy environment. Alterations to the environment can help, but that is not always possible, so children should also be supported to recognise their own state, and to learn and implement calming strategies until they can use these independently.

Think about times when you have felt close to the edge, wound up and ready to burst. What factors led you to that state? Anger? Frustration? Fear? Even some adults can become like helpless children in the face of a particularly fierce-looking spider. Was anything happening at that time that made it more difficult for you to remain calm, such as tiredness, illness or a particularly stressful situation in your life? What strategies did you use to pull yourself back from the edge? Perhaps you took deep breaths, removed yourself from the situation for a moment, or counted to ten in your head. As adults, we can often overcome strong emotions with rational thinking and learned calming strategies, but some children do not yet have that capacity. And anyway, if we do tip over the edge and completely lose it, rational, logical thinking evades us, and instinctive fight–flight–freeze responses take over. When that happens, we might look back on our actions in the cool light of day and feel ashamed of ourselves. Children are no different, but for children who have experienced trauma, that feeling of shame can become toxic, driving them even further into the very behaviours that caused their shame in the first place.

Remembering times when we as adults have felt ourselves dangerously close to losing control can help us to empathise with children who find themselves in the same state and are unable to pull themselves back. The goal should always be to prevent such outbursts through a combination of managing the child's environment, and supporting the child to learn to recognise their internal state and respond with calming strategies to regulate themselves.

Sometimes, there is a relatively obvious and immediate trigger to a child's outburst. It may be that they are overloaded with sensory information and a meltdown results from a long period of managing that overload. Much of the time, though, there is no obvious trigger, or the trigger seems too mild to have provoked such a serious response. A child who has not developed a healthy stress response system may be running 'hot' most of the time, and it will not take much to tip them over the edge into a fight–flight–freeze response. A teasing comment from another child, panic about not being able to complete their work on time, or feeling out of control over an impending transition might be enough. For some children, anger and lashing out are learned responses, almost habitual. They may have lived, or still be living, in an environment where violence and aggression are the norm, and have internalised these responses in the absence of any other model.

It can be helpful to keep a log of incidents, making notes on what was happening when the incident occurred, what triggers might have been present, and what the child said about the incident, to build up a fuller picture of possible triggering events and situations. Regular communications with parents and carers can provide valuable information about issues that may lead to increased stress, such as a poor night's sleep, or an unsettled period in the family home.

Where it is possible to spot signs of mounting anxiety and stress in a child, an adult can sometimes intervene to de-escalate the situation before it becomes explosive. Restlessness, fast breathing, clenched fists, a tense body posture, increased noise and chatter, rapid or high-pitched speech, clenched jaw, whining, crying, stubbornness and regressive behaviours like that of a much younger child can all be signs of mounting anxiety. Ideally, a child can be helped to learn to spot those signs in themselves, and begin to understand what is happening when rage rises. Dr Daniel Siegel's (2010) Hand Model of the Brain is an excellent visual tool for supporting even young children to understand the importance of using calming strategies to engage the thinking part of their brain.

The hope for all children who struggle with explosive outbursts is that they will eventually be able to learn to manage their own emotional responses. The operative word here is 'learn'. Although consequences may be appropriate depending on the situation, the consequences themselves will not teach the child what they need to know about managing themselves. It will take patient work from all the adults in the child's life acting as co-regulators and reinforcing the use of effective strategies before the child is fully equipped to manage alone.

Approaches to try

- Ensure that your body posture, facial expression and tone are calm and non-threatening. Model the behaviour that you want the child to adopt.

- Take slow deep breaths. This will help you remain calm, and the child may begin to breathe in line with your pattern.

- Maintain everybody's personal space. Getting too close to a child on the verge of explosion can be perceived as an aggressive move and can escalate the situation.

- It is fruitless to try to reason with an angry child when the thinking part of their brain is not engaged. Threatening them with consequences or trying to reason away their feelings will have no effect. Avoid dismissing or minimising their concerns, and instead narrate what you see in a low and even tone of voice. For example, 'I can see that you are feeling very frustrated right now.'

- Use phrases that move things on without making demands. For instance, 'It can be hard to stay calm when someone else takes the equipment that you wanted. Maybe there's another glue stick that you can use.'

- Pause between interactions and directions to give the child time to respond. It will take them longer to process what you are saying if they are in a heightened state. Count slowly to seven in your head before repeating your request or direction.

- Distraction techniques can engage a child's thinking brain by causing them to focus on something else, such as something they can see out of the window.

- Providing sensory input, such as a crunchy or chewy snack, or a short burst of intense physical activity can sometimes short-circuit a fight–flight–freeze response as it develops.

- Ensure that the child is not verbally or physically backed into a corner. Sometimes a child can back themselves into a corner and then we need to metaphorically or physically move aside to give the child an opportunity to change direction. If a child feels trapped, they are likely to escalate.

- Remain calm and in control, or at least convincingly give that impression. Seeing that the adult is unflappable can calm the fear that might be at the root of an angry response.

- Give the child choices about what will happen next, repeating them as often as necessary to avoid being drawn into secondary issues, which are only distractions from the main difficulty. If you have asked the child to give you their mobile phone, for instance, and eventually they comply, it will not be helpful to then take them to task because of the manner in which they complied. That might be a conversation for another, calmer time.

- Aggressive outbursts in the classroom raise the stress levels of everybody, including the teacher, so ensure that you are using your own preferred strategies for remaining calm and regulated, such as deep breathing.

- Have a plan of action for if a situation begins to get out of hand. Know who you will call to support you, and how you will maintain the safety of others in the room.

- If an aggressive child needs to be removed from the room, ensure that they are removed to an environment where they can be supported to become regulated. If they are unable to regulate themselves when you are in the room helping them, they are unlikely to manage it sitting alone on a chair outside the head teacher's office.

- Consequences can come later, and they should be proportionate to what has happened. It is more the certainty that such behaviour will not go unchallenged than the severity of the consequence that will be effective in most cases. Natural consequences work best whenever possible, as they encourage the building of cause-and-effect thinking.

- Once the incident passes, repair and rebuild. If possible, explore with the child what was happening and, together, consider alternative approaches to resolving the issue in future. This is the time to make it clear to the child that violent behaviour is always unacceptable.

- Aggressive outbursts will raise the tension level of everybody in the classroom. Acknowledge this after the event, and give everybody a few moments breathing space. If appropriate, gentle humour can break the tension, as long as it is not at the expense of the child who was struggling.

Rudeness and arguing

Whether it's picking arguments with other children or staff, disagreeing with everything someone says, or just a lack of basic manners, rude and argumentative behaviour can be frustrating and disruptive. A child may make offensive or personal comments (sometimes followed by a claim that they are only joking), call other people names, respond in a rude or cheeky way to reasonable questions, pointlessly say 'no' to inconsequential requests, or seem to go out of their way to provoke an argument. All of these things are difficult for staff and children to manage, and the mood of the classroom can be seriously adversely affected, especially if others rise to the bait and join in with the argument.

Like some other unwanted behaviours, rudeness and argumentativeness can be learned responses for children who have lived, or are living now, in environments where those forms of communication are the norm. All children benefit from having expectations around appropriate communication clearly spelled out and modelled by adults, and there are times when a gentle word of correction, privately delivered, will enable a child to understand that their rudeness is not acceptable.

However, if the root of the behaviour is control, fear or shame, then children will need an approach that acknowledges these underlying factors. Children who have had negative experiences of relationships with adults may have developed a survival strategy of keeping all adults at arm's length. Rudeness can be an excellent way to achieve this. Rudeness and argumentative talk can have the effect of undermining the teacher's authority, allowing the child to feel in control and powerful. Again, this may be a learned survival mechanism. Unhealthy feelings of shame can also provoke arguments and rude comments. If a child feels shamed, especially in front of an audience of peers, they can often respond angrily in an attempt to deflect those feelings of shame. Someone who will accept a quiet correction delivered in private may respond with arguments and aggressive talk if that same correction was delivered in front of their class mates as they try to save face and mask their shame and embarrassment.

Children who have difficulty reading social situations, or who lack empathy, may simply not realise that their comments, arguments, pointed suggestions or fault-finding can be offensive to others, especially if they are operating at a younger emotional age than their chronological age. They may lack the ability to link another's upset or frustration with what they have just said or done. If a child suddenly becomes rude and argumentative in the context of a previously good relationship with a teacher, it could be indicative of the child's fear of being rejected, or an attempt to test whether this adult will stick around for the long term, or give up when the going gets tough, especially if a major transition is looming. Some children need us to prove our commitment to them time and time again.

Approaches to try

- Once a child has drawn you into their argument, then they are in control. Avoid rising to the bait. Stick to stating your request or expectations and don't allow yourself to be sidetracked.

- If the child is muttering under their breath or speaking as an aside to another student, calmly ask them to repeat what they just said as if you genuinely didn't hear it. Sometimes they will think better of it on second thoughts and retreat. Then you can get on with your lesson, and speak to them about the incident in private later. If they do repeat it, then you can deal with it more directly.

- In a light tone of voice, suggest that the child has another go at saying what they want to say, but using different words.

- Be aware of what the child is doing, as well as what they are saying. They may sound rude or argumentative, while still complying with what you have asked them to do. Consider whether their attitude is something that needs to be addressed right now, or can be left until a later, calmer point.

- Refer frequently to aspects of your classroom code of conduct that relate to respecting one another, providing examples, and praising individuals when they act in a respectful manner.

- Address any underlying issues, such as fear or control issues caused by impending transitions, deadlines, perceived difficulty of the task or activity or similar.

- Try to see and accept the child's point of view, even if you don't agree with it. Things often seem unfair to children, and acknowledging those feelings neutrally may help to defuse an argument.

Lying

It is not terribly unusual for a child to tell a lie to get themselves out of trouble, and most teachers will have experienced that at some point. However, some children take this idea of lying for self-protection to an unreasonable degree, refusing to tell the truth when the evidence of their misdemeanour is staring everybody in the face, and even making up stories about somebody else being to blame. Toxic shame can be at the root of this behaviour. Where most children might accept that they have done something wrong, feel bad about it for a while, but accept the consequences and move on, a child who believes themselves to be worthless and innately bad may experience unbearable shame when caught out in even a minor wrongdoing. These children don't feel bad for a moment, they feel bad all the time, and cannot move on from these conflicts. Lying can be a way to protect themselves against their own strong negative feelings. The more they are backed into a corner, the more vigorously they defend themselves. This is when defensive behaviour can flip into attacking behaviour.

This kind of flat-out refusal to tell the truth can also be a defence mechanism learned early. If the consequences of being caught out doing something naughty have previously been extreme, a child may struggle to trust any adult enough to tell the truth. It is natural for a child to be afraid of adults if the adults in their lives have screamed at them, lost control, been violent towards them or rejected them, and it can take many years of patient consistency from trustworthy adults to help a child to overcome these fears.

Lying can also take the form of elaborate story-telling, where a child relates a supposedly true tale that is actually fabricated. The story may begin with a grain of truth, and then become exaggerated out of all recognition. Sometimes these lies are so transparent that even the other children recognise them as untrue, and may respond by shunning the child who tried to trick them. Often, fabrications will take the form of stories designed to exaggerate a child's achievements, or paint them as a hero. They may claim to have scored ten goals in the football match, rescued their classmates from an attacker, or been awarded a non-existent prize or award. The child is trying to manage others' opinions of them, rescue themselves from a situation where they feel vulnerable, or make themselves feel strong and in control, and it may simply not occur to them that the adult can usually easily check the facts for themselves.

A child's story-telling can also paint them as a victim, and this can become serious if their story relates to an issue of safeguarding. A child may make an allegation or tell a 'sob story' in order to deflect from the shame they are experiencing as a result of being caught out in a misdemeanour, to strengthen a relationship with an adult they perceive as sympathetic, or to try to avoid returning home or going to a specific teacher if they suspect they might be in trouble for something when they get there. Lack of empathy or undeveloped cause-and-effect thinking may mean that the child is unaware of the potentially serious consequences of what they have said. In her book, *The A–Z of Therapeutic Parenting* (2018), Sarah Naish recounts an incident where her son was caught stealing batteries from a shop. He was taken to his youth worker, who had a sympathetic approach. Anxious to keep her on his side and avoid the consequences of his theft, he embellished a tale whereby he stole the batteries to put in his torch, which he needed because there was no electricity in his bedroom. As a result of this, professionals visited the family home, where they found a comfortable and well-lit bedroom. His intention was not to cause a safeguarding panic, but to protect himself from the consequences of his actions, and the accompanying shame.

Allegations that children make must be taken seriously. Even children who seem to be habitual liars may be telling the truth if they make an allegation, whether it is one of abuse or neglect caused by an adult, or bullying caused by another child, and it is never safe to dismiss them. However, when working with children who have experienced historical trauma, abuse and neglect, there remains the possibility that current allegations may be rooted in past experiences, and this should be borne in mind during any action taken once an allegation has been made. Maintaining long-term and close relationships with parents, carers and other professionals involved in the child's life will provide much-needed context to any investigation. The lives of some carers and adoptive parents have been torn apart by what have later turned out to be false allegations, but abuse and neglect, sadly, can still occur in any family, and it will take expert professional support to manage allegations made by a child with a history of trauma.

Approaches to try

- Take time to consider the cause of the lying. Your response may differ depending on what the motivation for lying appears to have been.

- If a child is lying as a defensive behaviour, it is usually pointless to insist that they tell the truth right then, and attempts to do so will only escalate the situation. State that you will come back to the conversation later, and in private.

- Conversations about defensive lying need to be had away from an audience. It is possible that a child may be more willing to at least partially back down from their position if there is no risk of being shamed publicly.

- For lies that are essentially exaggerated story-telling, a first step might be to under-react to the story, and re-direct the conversation in a different direction. It is not necessary to contradict the child immediately.

- If exaggerations and fantasy stories continue to be a problem, a gentle correction may help. With a light tone, invite the child to try the story again, more realistically this time.

- Give the child an opportunity to correct their lie without pressure or fear of reprisals. Suggest that you will come back to the conversation in a few minutes, and if the child wants to 'change their mind', they can. If the child has responded in the heat of the moment without a thought to the consequences, they may be glad of an opportunity to put things straight.

- Avoid being drawn into an argument.

- Engage the child in activities to reduce their stress and anxiety so that they can make the right choice about telling the truth. Focused breathing or short bursts of physical activity can help.

- Ensure that communications with parents and carers are regular, and that their frequency increases during periods when a child's behaviour is more extreme than usual. This will support fact-checking, and also be invaluable in the case of an allegation being made.

- Investigate all allegations according to your setting's policy, but be aware that false allegations can occur when a child has a history of trauma.

- If a child makes a false allegation against you, try to remember that the child probably does not fully understand the potentially devastating consequences of their actions and may be acting only out of an overwhelming desire to protect themselves, rather than to hurt you. Keep accurate records of any incidents that occur so that the facts are on record should an allegation be made later. Adhere to safeguarding procedures at all times.

The silent treatment, quiet defiance and stubborn refusals

While some children's natural response to stress or anxiety is to be louder, more disruptive and more demanding, others respond by turning in on themselves. Avoidant children may appear withdrawn and quiet, avoid interactions with adults, fail to ask for help even when in serious difficulty, and deny that they are having any problems when asked. Children like this can respond to any increase in stress by shutting down completely, zoning out and dissociating. In the classroom, avoidant behaviour can look like refusing to respond to direct questions, refusing to make eye contact, inability to be cajoled out of an apparently sullen mood, daydreaming, not participating in tasks, not reacting at all when asked to do something or stop doing something, and appearing stubborn and defiant without necessarily being openly argumentative or outwardly disruptive. All of these behaviours may come as a surprise from a child who usually appears happy and compliant at school, but they are signs of underlying stress or anxiety driven by feelings of being unsafe. Once the child is home, this stress may spill out as meltdowns or aggression, leading parents and school staff to have a very different impression of the capabilities of the same child.

For our oldest, particularly, the energy they expend 'keeping it together' at school goes unnoticed, obstructs their learning and leaves anger and exhaustion for home life.

Increasing feelings of safety and security will be important in helping the avoidant child to express their needs and feelings, and to relax enough to respond to direct requests and questions from the teacher. If the child has not heard, or not understood the original request, they may respond by simply doing nothing and trying to remain invisible, hoping nobody notices their difficulty. Similarly, if the child feels unable to complete the activity, perhaps due to a low estimate of their own ability or over-estimating the difficulty of the task, they may simply opt out altogether. If a child regularly appears to be 'absent', it may be that they are dissociating. This can be a response to serious trauma, and may need professional interventions. Watch out for a child zoning out, not remembering what was said or what happened, switching between age-appropriate behaviour and regression to toddler or baby behaviour, sudden changes in facial expression with no apparent reason, fixed staring, lack of awareness of surroundings, lack of response to pain and being unaware of wetting or soiling. Pathological Demand Avoidance (PDA) may also be a consideration (see Chapter 2).

Approaches to try

- Check that an unresponsive child has both heard and understood what you said. Moving slightly closer to the child, being careful to display non-threatening body language, and re-stating or re-phrasing the original request in a low tone might help.

- IF PDA is suspected, try phrasing requests using language which does not imply a demand. For instance, instead of 'Tidy your books away now' try 'We won't be able to do the painting with those books all over your desk.'

- Avoidant children need opportunities to be brought into safe relationships. Consider buddying and nurture groups.

- Working in small groups or one to one can reduce the pressure to respond in front of the whole class.

- Make a conscious effort to notice the child who often goes unnoticed, in a positive way. For instance, quietly acknowledge when you see them working hard. Make this praise low key and as private as possible.

- Provide alternative ways for the child to indicate that they need help or want to ask a question. For instance, they could place a coloured card on their desk. Make sure they know that you are available to help them if they need it.

- If a silent or withdrawn child has a classroom assistant or key adult with them, allow this other adult to act as an intermediary. The child can say their answers or comments quietly to the intermediary who can then write them on a small whiteboard for the teacher to see later.

- Give the child space. Sometimes if a child is really overwhelmed, they need the adult to step back and give them time to calm and respond.

Running and hiding

Hiding under a table or in the toilets can be an extension of the same avoidant behaviour discussed previously. While a more outwardly expressive child might respond to fear or stress by shouting, screaming, crying, becoming angry or aggressive, an avoidant child may simply seek to remove themselves to a place of safety, either within their own mind, or in a physical location, closing themselves off from the world around them. Running away can be another avoidant response to anxiety, fear, shame or sensory overload brought on, for instance, by an impending transition, or as a result of an incident for which the child feels they will be blamed or punished.

When a child absconds from the classroom, or from the school grounds, they are often not thinking straight, but are acting in the heat of the moment, with no thought given to the consequences. This can be true even if the child appears outwardly calm, as if they are walking out as part of an act of defiance. Appealing to reason and logic is likely to have little effect. Shouting after the child, chasing them or cornering them are all actions that are likely to raise their stress levels further and escalate matters. For children who respond impulsively when stress levels are raised, it will be helpful to keep the environment as calm and safe as possible and put strategies in place to reduce overwhelming sensory input, fear of the unknown, loss of control, and the sense that events are spiralling towards an unpleasant conclusion. Running away can be a particular problem on school trips, when lack of the usual boundaries and structures combined with excitement, sensory stimulation and long periods sitting still for travel can all contribute to a flight response.

Approaches to try

- Plan transitions, beginnings and endings, making sure that the child knows exactly what will happen, to reduce the risk of anxiety around those times.

- Make use of calm rooms, or calm areas in the classroom to head off rising stress levels before they fully take hold.

- Use key adults to calm a hiding child. Sit in the hiding place with the child, as long as this is not likely to escalate the situation.

- Draft in extra supervision for school trips, activities that involve leaving the classroom, the start and end of the school day, and any other situation that has triggered running or hiding in the past.

- If a child runs away, stay as calm as possible and avoid shouting or chasing after them. For high-risk children, have a plan in place for dealing with running, named individuals who can intervene, and a system for calling for help.

- Rather than running after a child, try running with them if possible, speaking calmly. Attempt to match their pace, and then bring that pace down gradually.

- Once the hidden child is found, or the running child is standing still, avoid overwhelming them with lots of people, or with immediate consequences. Supporting members of staff can back away, leaving key adults to talk to the child. Conversation should be aimed at calming the child, rather than reasoning with them. When the child is able, take them to a comfortable, private space and provide a drink and a crunchy or chewy snack if possible. Thick drinks, like smoothies, sucked through a straw can help as sucking is regulating. Only when the child is fully calm should any conversation about the dangers or consequences of running and hiding take place.

Low-level disruption, chatter and noise

Every classroom seems to have its chatterbox characters who always have something to say and will easily be distracted from their work by the opportunity for a conversation. However, if a child's disruptive chatter goes beyond conversations with their friends or occasional calling out, then it's possible that the lasting effects of trauma and attachment difficulties are at play. Some children seem to make incessant noise, either through talking, singing or making nonsense sounds. They may continually ask the same questions even though they must know the answers, comment on everything that happens in the room, or repeat particular words and phrases over and over again.

Repetitive noise-making can be a form of verbal 'stimming', or self-stimulation. Rhythmic patterns of words, spoken or sung, can be soothing, as anybody who has sung or read nursery rhymes to small children will know. When they are stimming, children are not really trying to communicate anything; rather they are providing themselves with sensory input, and receiving comfort or a sense of calm from the sensation. Stimming is most commonly associated with autistic spectrum disorders, but in reality many people stim, perhaps by biting their nails, twirling their hair or drumming their fingers on the desk. Verbal stimming may be a sign of increased anxiety or sensory overload.

Most constant noise and chatter will not follow the repetitive, self-soothing pattern of stimming, however, and other causes need to be considered. A child with attachment difficulties may subconsciously use continual talking and noise as a way of making sure that they are not being forgotten by the important adult in the room, which can become a more urgent need at times of heightened anxiety such as transition times, when exams or tricky assignments are looming, or when other changes are taking place. Anxiety over change may cause children to ask the same questions over and over again, for instance, asking repeatedly for clarification about details of a forthcoming school trip.

Some children may seem over-reliant on the teacher, asking lots of questions about the task or activity, or frequently asking if they are doing their work right, or if their work is good. As long as they can monopolise the teacher's time and attention, then they can be sure that they are being held in the teacher's mind and will not be forgotten. Even acting as the class clown can be a way to maintain the focus of the teacher's attention on them. Children who behave like this will often be seen as attention-seeking, but these behaviours can more accurately be described as 'attachment-seeking'.

Fundamentally, they are more interested in the adults in the classroom and the state of their relationships with those adults than they are with whatever work they are supposed to be doing.

When children have developmental delay, or gaps in their social and emotional development, they can often seem to function like a much younger child as they struggle with impulsivity and lack of cause-and-effect thinking. Calling out inappropriately, or having difficulties containing their thoughts within their own heads could be a result of a child simply not yet having learned the social and behavioural norms of the school environment. Think about the content of the child's chatter. Is it really more like the conversation of a much younger child? If so, the child will need to be supported according to their social and emotional age, rather than their chronological age.

Approaches to try

- Warn children in advance of any changes, prepare well for transitions using visual timetables as appropriate, and do everything possible to lower anxiety around anything that is out of their normal routine.

- Set clear expectations around what you want the child to do before they come to speak to you again, but make the goals small and quickly achievable. For example, tell the child that you want them to complete three questions before they bring their work to show you again.

- Place attachment-seeking children close to your desk, and in your eyeline, so that you can easily make eye contact and demonstrate that you have not forgotten them through non-verbal signals such as a thumbs-up or a smile.

- Use the child's name frequently to show that they are held in your mind even if you are sometimes busy elsewhere.

- If chattering and asking questions is an attachment-seeking behaviour, ignoring the child will only exacerbate it as it will reinforce their inner belief that they will be forgotten. Always acknowledge that the child is speaking, even if it is only to indicate that they need to wait and you will come to them in a moment.

- Provide the child with an alternative way to attract your attention, such as a little flag to put up on the desk. Always acknowledge the appearance of the flag, even if your response is only to reassure the child that you will be with them after you finish your current task, or in two minutes.

- Ask the child to write down what they want to say. They are unlikely to write a stream of nonsense chatter, but the act of putting pen to paper may be enough of a distraction to stop them from talking.

Stealing and damaging property

Children can damage their own and others' property by accident, or deliberately. Accidents caused by heavy-handedness may be a result of poor proprioceptive awareness making the child unaware of how much pressure and strength they are using, or be symptomatic of dyspraxia. Sensory issues can also be the cause of children scratching, chewing, biting and fiddling with objects, clothes and even furniture, until they break or become damaged beyond repair. Sometimes accidental damage occurs because children lack cause-and-effect thinking. It may simply not occur to a child that balancing that breakable item on top of a wobbly pile of books is likely to lead to disaster; the same lack of cause-and-effect thinking means that they don't learn a lesson from that experience, and so go on to do the same thing again tomorrow.

Deliberate damage is more complex. Noting what else was happening, and what the child's emotional state appeared to be at the time of the incident might provide context. A child in a heightened state of emotions may damage property in the heat of the moment, without any real intent behind it except as a way to express their strong feelings. In that case, managing the child's environment to reduce their stress and anxiety may reduce the frequency and severity of incidents (see 'Angry outbursts and violence' earlier in this chapter). If a child has been used to living in an environment where violent responses are commonplace and items are often broken or damaged, they may not grasp the value of objects, either financially, or sentimentally.

In some ways, it is perhaps easier to rationalise and understand the behaviour of a child who damages something in what seems to be a temporary lapse due to strong emotions. It is not acceptable, but at least it is something most of us could empathise with to some extent. Children who coolly and apparently deliberately smash, break and damage their own or others' property are much harder to understand and to empathise with. Why might this happen? Even if a child appears to be in control of their actions, it is still possible for their behaviour to be driven by strong, underlying emotional responses, learned through trauma. A child may have a strong need to evoke a response from anybody around them in order to ensure that they are being held in mind, even if this response is framed in negative terms. Children who have been terrified and powerless will sometimes go to great lengths to feel in control and powerful, lacking the ability to empathise with the impact that their actions might have on others. This can become a factor if another child is receiving a lot of attention, praise or rewards, or if an interaction with a child or an adult has left them feeling overwhelming shame.

Children who have experienced trauma will also sometimes destroy or damage their own possessions, and even their most treasured items. The causes of this behaviour can be complex, but can include feeling that they do not deserve nice things and being unable to manage the internal conflict this causes. Often, even natural consequences seem to have little effect. If a child destroys, say, their tablet, the natural consequence is that they have no tablet to use, but the child might subvert this by insisting that the tablet was rubbish anyway, and they don't care if they don't have it anymore. This is likely to be bravado designed to mask their shame and loss, and should not necessarily be taken at face value.

While it is not uncommon for children to occasionally take something that is not theirs, if it persists, and is not corrected by conversations, or appropriate sanctions, stealing can be an indicator of underlying difficulties. Persistent stealing is similar to damaging property in that it can be a symptom of the child feeling out of control, jealousy of another person who appears more fortunate and favoured, lacking empathy and cause-and-effect thinking, and self-sabotage. A child may damage or steal the property of someone they have an attachment relationship with (such as their key adult) because of feelings of anger towards them, or because they are afraid of the developing relationship and need to sabotage it in some way. Children who have experienced neglect and sudden removal from their families may steal in order to get things that they think will make them feel better inside, or to collect objects that might become useful in some way in an unknowable future. Deep down, they may feel as though they themselves were stolen, and taking something from others gives them momentary relief for their inner state. For some children, stealing food may have been the difference between eating and going hungry and, even if they are taken to a home where food is plentiful, it is very hard for them to accept that they no longer need to be responsible for their own survival. There are many reasons why a child may not have internalised the understanding that property has boundaries, and taking other people's things is wrong and hurtful. Developmental delay can result in this understanding coming much later in life than it might for others, and children who have experienced even their own physical boundaries being utterly violated by sexual or physical abuse may be unable to naturally grasp or value the importance of boundaries around other people and their possessions.

As children get older, peer pressure to fit in, and to have what others have, intensifies. For a child who already feels different and 'other' due to their background or legal status, or whose family circumstances are such that they cannot access those must-have items, the temptation to steal can be strong. This is true of many children but, for those who lack cause-and-effect thinking and empathy, and who may not value being seen as 'good' or trustworthy, these temptations can easily lead to action with little thought to the consequences. Children who, because of developmental immaturity, cannot safely be given access to things that their peers enjoy, such as smart phones, or pocket money, may feel this jealousy particularly sharply. Depending on what the child does with the items they have stolen, persistent stealing, especially with a relatively sudden onset, can also be an indicator of drug or alcohol problems.

Approaches to try

- Maintain regular communications between school and home about incidents of property damage or stealing. If this is a problem at school, it is likely to be a problem at home as well. Such communications will aid both the school and parents and carers with fact-checking if a child suddenly 'loses' or acquires an item.

- Use natural consequences, such as doing without broken items, or contributing to the replacement or repair of damaged and broken items where possible. Even if this seems not to work in the short term, the aim is to develop cause-and-effect thinking over time. Consistent, predictable, natural consequences work best. It is more likely that a child will eventually learn from the connection between smashing their calculator and having no calculator to use in Maths lessons, than it is that they will learn from the rather tenuous connection between smashing their calculator and sitting in detention.

- Ensure that high-value and potentially dangerous items are secured in the classroom. Avoid leaving your personal possessions unattended.

- Make a note of items stolen by a child so that any patterns can be identified. It may be that stealing is focused around, say, food, or small high-value items. Parents or carers may be able to assist with understanding the underlying cause of automatic stealing behaviours.

- Wonder aloud about the underlying need that may have led to the damage or theft. For instance, 'I wonder if you hid Clara's new glitter gel pen because you felt angry that she had one and you don't?' These conversations can lead children into a better vocabulary for identifying and naming their feelings, which is a prerequisite for learning to recognise them and find different ways of dealing with them.

- Making a child say 'Sorry' can be an unsatisfactory experience for everybody involved, especially if it is clear that there is little genuine feeling behind the words. Focus on restitution, where the child who has damaged or stolen another's property actively does something to make amends, such as tidying their locker space, or taking over one of their jobs for a day. This will work best if the child who did the damage offers the suggestion.

- Increase activities designed to nurture the child and strengthen attachment relationships.

- Consider sensory solutions such as chewy bracelets and necklaces, or fiddle toys, for children who damage things by biting, chewing and fiddling with them.

- Follow your school's safeguarding procedures if you suspect that a child's stealing is part of a pattern of behaviour associated with drug or alcohol abuse. Similarly, if a child suddenly has access to high-value items that you suspect they could not have acquired legitimately, consider the possibility that they could be a victim of child sexual exploitation and take action according to safeguarding procedures if necessary.

Over-reacting, crying and whining

In any classroom there will be children who seem more sensitive to what might be considered the normal rough and tumble of everyday life. These are children who may appear shy or timid, unwilling to participate in new things, easily tired or quickly upset, prone to emotional collapse, tears and meltdowns. This is not usually a result of a disorder, and psychologist Elaine Aron suggests that highly sensitive people may make up 15–20 per cent of the population. Aron has published a number of books on the subject, of which perhaps the most well-known is *The Highly Sensitive Child* (2015). She describes highly sensitive children as taking in more sensory information than other children, becoming over-stimulated and tiring quickly, and so being more likely to experience sudden meltdowns and tantrums.

Many children who have experienced trauma, abuse and neglect are similarly highly sensitive to their environments. It may be that they are hyper-vigilant and always on the alert for potential danger, so that they are continually taking in and processing sensory information, jumping or startling at the slightest unexpected sound or movement. Those who have learned that to be visible, to be noticed, is the safest route to ensuring their needs are met, may habitually make every drama into a crisis, ensuring that the adults around them are focused on them and their needs. These behaviours are learned from infancy and are a kind of reflex response, not always within the child's direct control. Children who are primed for danger may struggle to tell the difference between actual and imagined risk, and so may react strongly to images, stories, films and safety information that other children take in their stride.

My adopted son was about six when he read about a burglar in a children's story. He became obsessed with the possibility of someone coming into the house to take our things, and insisted on watching me lock all the doors every night before he went to bed. He talked about burglars all the time and if anything was lost, assumed that someone had stolen it. This fear developed to the point that he wouldn't go to sleep in his bedroom unless I was also there to protect him from burglars.

It is tempting to tell sensitive and fearful children to 'Get over it' or 'Toughen up', or to compare them to their peers negatively in an attempt to encourage them to have some perspective, but doing so risks filling a child with shame over a behaviour that they cannot, at this point, control. There is benefit in gently supporting a child to learn about relative risk, and to manage their own emotional state when faced with difficult or upsetting incidents. In the case of the child who was afraid of burglars, it was wise of the parent to allow the child to see and experience the security measures in the home that were designed to keep everybody safe.

Over-reacting to minor incidents and injuries can be a cause for concern if it leads to implications for safeguarding. Take the example where you, as the teacher, lightly brush past a child in the corridor and their response is to cry out and claim that you almost knocked them over. Such accusations can seem unjust and personal, raising stress levels and provoking fear of investigations and recriminations. Responding to these claims in the heat of the moment by arguing that you never did any such thing is only likely to escalate the situation and draw an unhelpful audience. Children with sensory issues may genuinely experience a light touch more intensely than others. Children who have been physically hurt by adults in the past may react strongly to a minor incident out of fear that they will be hurt again and inability to predict the motives and intentions of adults. It is not necessarily the case that the child is deliberately trying to get an adult into trouble.

Whining or complaining about minor incidents and imagined or inconsequential injuries and illnesses can also have its roots in early trauma. For children who do not have a healthy blueprint for forming attachment relationships, a mystery 'stomach ache' or a story about someone being 'mean' may seem a completely logical way to draw adults towards them to bring the nurture they crave. This litany of real or imagined problems will keep adults close and ensure that the child feels important and the centre of somebody's attention, at least for a time. Eventually, most adults will begin to find this behaviour wearing and withdraw. A child's response to withdrawal may simply be to increase the attachment-seeking behaviour, since they have no other reliable model for how relationships are supposed to work and yet they crave relationship. Alternatively, they may turn their attentions to somebody new, and begin all over again. While it is important not to allow unhealthy dependent relationships to build up between children and staff, attempting to avoid them by cutting children off from staff members they seem close to, or rotating staff regularly to avoid relationships developing, will not support the child to overcome attachment-seeking behaviours. Adults need to model and demonstrate healthy attachments to children, and this can only be done within the context of a relationship.

Some children seem to whine and complain about every task they are given. They may say they are too tired, or grumble about some piece of equipment they do not have, or huff and puff over the work itself, saying that it is too hard, even though, as the teacher, you know that it is well within their capabilities. These may be procrastination strategies and can be used to mask difficulties such as fear of attempting an unfamiliar task, uncertainty about what to do because the child has not heard or understood the instructions, or fear of shame if they fail to complete the task properly. Children might also procrastinate in this way over participating in activities that signal a transition is underway, such as tidying away at the end of a lesson. This can be especially true if the child is unsure about what is coming next. See Chapter 7 for strategies to effectively manage difficult transitions.

Approaches to try

- Ensure that fearful children are aware of the measures taken by the school to keep them safe. This does not need to be oppressive or over-stated. It can be as low key as simply mentioning in passing that, for instance, the gates are always locked during the day, or nobody can come into the building without pressing the buzzer and signing in at the office.

- Where possible, consider filtering stories, films and curriculum materials for issues that might make a vulnerable child excessively fearful, or at least communicate with parents and carers in advance of covering such material (see Chapter 8 for strategies on managing sensitive material in school).

- Respond to whining and complaints neutrally, and avoid being drawn into secondary issues, especially when procrastination is the likely cause.

- Encourage children to re-frame their problem as a solution. For example, instead of complaining, 'I can't find my pencil!' the child can ask the teacher if they might borrow a pencil.

- Ignoring attachment-seeking in children is likely to intensify the behaviour. Respond calmly and neutrally, even if it is only to say that you will speak to them when you have finished what you are doing.

- Maintain good home–school communications so everybody is on the same page when it comes to imaginary or inflated illnesses, or reports of staff, parents or other children bullying or being mean.

- Keep a log of incidents so that you have the facts at hand should an investigation be needed later.

- Keep records of children who frequently visit the school nurse, or the office, or who are often sent home because of illness. Examine the records for signs of any pattern, such as illness occurring at the same time of day, during a particular lesson such as PE, or in clusters at certain times of the year. This may give clues as to any underlying cause or anxiety.

- Be aware that anxiety can cause physical symptoms that may be interpreted by a child as 'feeling sick' or having 'a headache'.

Chapter 11

OUTSIDE SPACES

In this chapter:

Unstructured free time

Moving around school

Bullying and peer relationships

Food issues

Toilet troubles

A significant proportion of the school day is spent outside of the boundaries of the classroom environment, whether it is moving between classes in corridors, outside in play areas, or in the dining area. During these times, children may be less closely supervised, in the care of non-teaching staff who may not be as familiar to them or with their needs, and surrounded by crowds of other noisy, moving children. In their *Bridging the Gap* report (2018), Adoption UK highlighted the results from a survey of adopted parents which found that 60 per cent of their children experience particular difficulties at school during breaks and lunchtimes. This demonstrates the need for all school staff, not just classroom staff, to be included in training on attachment and trauma, and to be involved in implementing strategies put in place to support individual children.

Effectively managing transitions from class time to free time, and at the start and end of the day is one vital aspect of supporting children who have particular difficulties outside the classroom that can sometimes spill over into classroom time. Strategies for managing transitions are discussed in more detail in Chapter 7.

Unstructured free time

Perhaps we take it for granted that all young children know how to play. Indeed, most children will arrive at primary school with the necessary basic social skills required for interactive play, such as awareness of turn-taking, of collaborating, and of following the rules of the game, even if they slip up occasionally. However, children with gaps in their development, whose pre-school education may have been disrupted or non-existent, or who have not had play modelled at home, can fall behind in these soft skills. Children who have experienced trauma or disrupted attachments may operate at a much younger level than their chronological age might suggest, and it is not uncommon for them to choose to play with the younger children in the school even as they move up the year groups towards Years 5 and 6. If children are excluded from play opportunities, either by other children, or because they simply give up trying, then it is unlikely that they will develop the skills needed to participate, and the gap between them and their peers will only widen.

These developmental gaps and delays can be accompanied by sensory processing difficulties which make the hustle and bustle of a noisy playground something of an ordeal, especially in contrast to the orderly, mostly quiet environment of their classroom. Hyper-vigilant children have much more work to do, scanning every sound and movement for signs of danger, and children with ineffective stress response systems are likely to respond dramatically to minor provocations such as jostling or a funny look from another child. Children who are hypo-sensitive to proprioceptive and vestibular stimulation may use playground time as an opportunity to seek out sensory input by running, twirling and crashing.

A common and understandable response to a child engaging in unwanted and inappropriate behaviour during break times is to keep them inside, under supervision. However, a struggling child will never learn to manage a situation they are not exposed to, and removal of essential opportunities to run off steam, enjoy fresh air and natural light, and forget any tensions from the previous lesson is likely to result in increasingly challenging behaviour in the classroom, especially for a child with sensory difficulties. Adjustments may need to be made to include a child in free-time activities, and adult input may be needed to provide guidance and support, and to watch for signs of situations going out of control, intervening before crisis point is reached.

As children grow older, developmental gaps between them and their peers can tend to widen. While the other teenagers might prefer to spend their free time talking or 'hanging out', some may still need considerable supervision and guidance if they are to navigate break times without incident. Older children with sensory difficulties or heightened levels of anxiety or stress may still benefit from involvement in physical activities to help regulate them, and, where their peers are not naturally involved, this may not happen without encouragement and organisation from supervising staff.

Approaches to try

- Provide supervised activities (inside or outside) that children can access if they struggle to manage free play or outside spaces. These are not punishments, but alternatives, and should be part of a strategy for building social and play skills.

- Involve supervising staff, or volunteers to provide structured play activities in the playground, and to support struggling children to participate appropriately in these activities. This could be as simple as organising a game of 'What time is it, Mr Wolf?' and does not necessarily need investment in expensive equipment.

- Actively teach playground games to all children – this can form part of PE lessons for younger children – and make a plan with supervisors to introduce them in the playground. If more children are engaged in structured games and activities, the opportunities for unfocused activities that can lead to conflict are reduced.

- Consider providing playground equipment to encourage children towards more structured physical activity. This is just as important for secondary school students as it is for young children. Sports and fitness equipment, climbing equipment, targets and other markings painted on hard surfaces, and games integrated into playground furniture are all ideas that might attract older children to make more productive use of their free time.

- Encourage children towards existing lunchtime extra-curricular activities. This not only provides structure and routine to unstructured time, but also encourages their sense of belonging and inclusion in the school community.

- Involve children in outside jobs, such as maintaining playground equipment, leaf-sweeping, or being the 'monitor'. These jobs should not be punishments, but preferably done alongside an adult.

- If outdoor spaces are very expansive, consider zoning them, with physical barriers between areas to reduce the scope for wild running. Zones could include a ball-game zone, a chill-out zone, a sensory zone or a nature area.

- Zone lining-up areas and walkways by using a different floor surface, or by painting lines on the hard surface. This gives children a visual reminder of where they should be and what their conduct should be in those spaces.

- Make sure children have what they need to make it easier for them to follow the rules. Are there enough litter bins? If children are not allowed to sit on window sills, steps or walls, is other appropriate seating provided?

- Involve older children as play leaders to encourage others to join in with organised games.

- If a child has a key adult, ensure that they check in with the child during unstructured times, even if it is just to say hello. The key adult is more likely to be able to quickly gauge a child's emotional or anxiety state and intervene if necessary.

- Maintain unvarying and predictable routines around the start and end of unstructured time.

Moving around school

Many of the difficulties children encounter when moving around school are similar to those of unstructured time: noise, crowds, reduced levels of supervision, anxiety around transition and physical jostling. The short space between one lesson and another also introduces a time pressure, especially in a large school with several buildings or some distance between classrooms. If the time between lessons in your school is barely enough for a child to visit the toilet, have a quick drink, and make it to their next lesson at the other end of the building on time, then the likelihood is that some children will be arriving at your classroom door stressed, or late.

Keeping to a timetable, and being in the right place at the right time with the right equipment, is a particular challenge for children with weak executive functioning skills. Timetables can be forgotten or lost, the layout of the school may be difficult to remember, and poor management of time might mean that they spend longer in the toilet than they meant to, making them late. An abrupt change from a quiet, orderly classroom to a busy, crowded corridor can cause a spike in anxiety for children always close to a fight–flight–freeze response, and the accompanying rise in sensory input only adds to this sensation.

> My daughter has mild cerebral palsy, sensory difficulties, poor working memory and executive functioning difficulties. The support her secondary school provided academically was excellent and we had no complaints about that, but outside of the classroom it was different. She was regularly lost or confused, and sometimes 15 minutes late to her lessons. Even when she was allowed more time to move between lessons, it wasn't enough because she was physically much slower than other children. The last straw came when she tripped over in a corridor and it was so crowded that other children literally stepped on her because they couldn't get out of the way in time.

Some children will explode from the classroom like a cork out of a bottle, with the instinct to run, bounce or twirl never far away. They may be seeking proprioceptive or vestibular input as a result of hypo-sensitivity to sensory input, but narrow, crowded corridors, or busy open spaces are far from ideal places to achieve this. Schools have 'no running' policies for good reason, and children who need more sensory input will benefit from being supported to get this in other, safer ways.

Approaches to try

- Ensure that the ends of lessons are on time, calm and follow a predictable routine so that children leave the room without needing to rush.

- Dismiss children from the classroom in small groups, such as table by table. Or make a little game of it by, for example, dismissing them according to what month their birthday is in, or according to which of them are displaying a particular desired behaviour. This stops a bottleneck at the classroom door, reducing sensory stress and the possibility of scuffles between children anxious to get out. Be aware that having to wait to get out of the room may increase some children's anxiety levels so it might be wise to include them in the first group.

- Ensure that facilities such as coat and bag storage areas, drinks machines or water fountains, and toilets are well supervised, and designed to minimise crowding and confusion.

- Be aware of the situation immediately outside of your classroom door as children are arriving to lessons. Even if the corridor is not particularly crowded, queuing children can cause an obstruction to those still walking past, either unintentionally or deliberately. Nervous younger students may find that walking past large queues of noisy Year 11 students increases their anxiety levels, even if the older students actually pose no threat.

- Allow individual children with specific needs to leave the classroom first, or even early, so that they are less likely to encounter large crowds and overwhelming sensory stimulation.

- Have a daily check-in with children whose executive functioning skills are weak to briefly go over their timetable for the day and talk them through the equipment they will need. Visual timetables can be helpful.

- Gather children's views on any problem areas in corridors and walkways. Children, if only because of their smaller stature, will often have a different perspective on the school environment to the adults who work there. Use their views to inform supervision plans and the development of strategies for improving out-of-classroom behaviour and routines.

- Refer to your classroom code of conduct frequently when reinforcing safe behaviour out of the classroom.

Bullying and peer relationships

Children with gaps in their development, who lack a coherent model for how to form and maintain friendships and other relationships, and who do not have the skills to engage in play, turn-taking and banter can have particular difficulties when it comes to making and keeping friends. If their behaviour towards others is avoidant, or unpredictable, or aggressive, other children will naturally withdraw from them.

> My foster daughter has no real friends at school. Although she is in Year 2, she prefers to play with Reception-aged children and struggles to get along with children her own age. Next year, she will have to play in the junior playground with children her own age and older. I just feel as though she's going to be miserable and lonely all the time.

Children with attachment difficulties may form intense friendships that quickly burn out as the other child becomes overwhelmed by the possessiveness involved. In these cases, a child may almost become fixated on that one particular friend, constantly talking about them, and exclusively spending time with them. They may even become controlling and manipulative as part of this dynamic. Others may struggle to make friends at all, lacking the social skills required, and putting others off with their awkward attempts to join in. For some children, lack of empathy or poor social skills may mean that they are unable to repair a relationship after even a minor disagreement or argument, and the friendship is permanently lost.

The implications of poor or non-existent peer relationships go beyond the playground. Who will that child sit with when the class is doing group or paired work if none of the other children want them in their group? Who will pick them for their team in PE lessons? Birthday parties that one child is conspicuously never invited to can easily become a source of shame and conflict that spills over into the classroom. Some parents and carers of traumatised children report that their children seem especially drawn to others with similar backgrounds. While a shared history and understanding can be a good foundation for a friendship, it can also result in the child gaining a partner in crime, so to speak, and be a source of huge worry for families.

> He is becoming aware of his learning problems (about two years behind his classmates). As he becomes older it is more obvious to other children, some of whom are picking on him because of it. If he's upset, he can't learn and is unhappy at school. We are worried that his progress will be further affected by this.

We know that insecurely attached children are more likely both to be bullied and to be bullies (Tough, 2012). Children with a background of complex trauma can be targets for bullying from other children for a number of reasons. They may behave like much younger children, be small in stature due to neglect or pre-birth trauma, engage in self-soothing behaviours, or just generally be different enough to attract unwelcome attention to themselves. For children who are living in neglectful or chaotic circumstances, lack of money, old or worn clothing or lack of hygiene may be enough to incite hurtful remarks from others. Adoptees and care-experienced young people have reported being bullied because of their legal status (Adoption UK, 2018).

Children who bully others are perhaps more difficult to empathise with. For children with a history of disrupted attachments and trauma, dominating others may stem from a need to protect themselves by being in charge and in control, or may be a maladaptive attempt to form relationships, without the benefit of a healthy internalised model for doing so. Lack of empathy or poor social skills may mean that a child who bullies perceives the behaviour of others to be hostile or challenging when it isn't, or that they don't realise that their actions towards others are hurtful. Like other aggressive behaviours, bullying behaviour can stem from a need to be noticed by teachers, or to be part of an 'in crowd' if, by bullying a particular classmate, the child feels that they will be fitting in with a powerful group of other children. Where a group is involved, joining in with bullying can be a protective mechanism, ensuring that the child is not the next victim of the group. In this situation, children may feel afraid to speak out against the behaviour and be going along with it unwillingly.

> His ability to form and maintain relationships was limited as he was drawn to kids who also wanted to bully him. This meant that he wasn't able to focus in class.

Approaches to try

- Assess whether the child actually has the skills needed to support peer relationships, such as turn-taking, sharing, language and communication proficiency in line with peers, ability to manage and resolve a conflict. If not, then allowing a child loose in the playground to make friends and be sociable is unlikely to achieve the desired result.

- Many traumatised children will need a high level of support to manage friendships and social situations. Ensure that the role of the key adult in drawing alongside the child and modelling and supporting social interactions is valued across the school.

- Provide close adult support in the playground to initiate and model social interactions. The adult should draw back for short periods to allow the child to practise their skills. As the child becomes more confident, the adult can draw back for longer and longer periods.

- Find an activity or game that the child is good at, and support them to invite other children to join them in it.

- Have a class project that involves trying something new and investigating everybody's opinions. Children who are struggling with peer relationships can take responsible roles such as collecting opinions, or presenting the results.

- Use buddying programmes in the playground. Some schools have introduced 'buddy benches' where children can sit if they are in need of a playmate, but be aware that avoidant children may find it too hard to put themselves forward in this way and will need actively supporting into schemes.

- Be aware that avoidant children will not necessarily reveal the extent of their distress. Although a child may seem to be 'fine' about an incident, or a comment from another child, they may be experiencing internal turmoil, fear, shame and anxiety. Parents and carers may have a different perspective on their child's responses to the situation.

- While it is not possible to force children to be friends, it is possible to manage the classroom environment so that particular children are not left out, sidelined or made to feel unwanted in group and paired activities.

- Help socially anxious children to make a plan for common social occurrences. Who will they speak to? What will they say? What are their fears? What strategies can they use to overcome those fears and calm themselves?

- Involve children in paired tasks that are low risk, such as asking the socially anxious child to pair with another, empathetic child in tidying the stationery cupboard.

- Ensure that anti-bullying programmes include topics on children's different legal and family statuses. Just as bullying on the grounds of race, disability or sexual orientation is unacceptable, so children should be helped to understand that bullying a child because they are adopted, or living in foster care, is equally unacceptable. Comments such as 'No wonder your real mum didn't want you' should be treated with the same seriousness as other forms of targeted abuse.

- For more general strategies on managing aggressive behaviour, see Chapter 10.

Food issues

Many children who have experienced trauma, neglect, abuse and disrupted attachments have a difficult relationship with food. This may be linked to past experiences of food insecurity, or an outward manifestation of another underlying difficulty. As a society, we have expectations around food and mealtimes. There is pressure to eat healthily, eat at certain times, avoid over-eating, share in lovely family meals, eat savoury food before treats, have nice table manners and so on. Everybody has expectations around food, but for children whose experiences of mealtimes have previously been chaotic, who have perhaps had to fend for themselves, lived for long periods without enough food or with unpredictable availability of food, or with no variety of food, the challenge of living up to these expectations can be enormous, and social norms may never have been learned.

Food issues can make lunchtimes and snack time a minefield. Children may hoard and steal food, eat food all at once, be unable to tell when they are hungry or full, obsess about when they will next get some food, be unable to cope with sharing food, binge on sugary food, be extremely picky eaters, eat until they make themselves sick, eat quickly without chewing, and have difficulties with certain textures of food. Food can also be an area where children can exercise control, refusing to eat, or holding items of food in their mouths until long after the mealtime is over.

Anxiety about food can stem from a history of food scarcity, or unpredictability of supply. Even if a child is now living in a home where food is plentiful and a variety of food is offered, learned anxieties about food are not easy to overcome. In school, this might mean that some children become anxious about when they will next be able to eat, what they can have, and where the food is, long before lunchtime, and if a child is focusing on where their next meal is coming from, they are not concentrating on their learning. The urge to secure their own food supply may lead them to hoard food in bags and lockers, steal food from other children, and eat their entire packed lunch in the first 30 minutes of the school trip, especially if they lack the cause-and-effect thinking to predict that this will leave them hungry later. If food is being shared, or given out to the class as a reward or treat, children with food anxiety are likely to be overwhelmed with the desire to ensure that they get what they need and are not forgotten. This can lead to them pushing other children out of the way to get to the front of the queue, over-filling their plates at buffet-style spreads, and grabbing more than what could reasonably be considered their fair share. These are survival instincts that are not wholly within the child's control in the heat of the moment.

Physiological results of trauma, abuse and neglect can also create difficulties around food. When our cortisol levels are high, we tend to crave sugar. For children whose cortisol levels are set high, hoarding, stealing and binging sugary foods can be a problem that is difficult to overcome. In some traumatised children, the important sense of interoception is not sufficiently developed. Interoception allows us to feel and understand the sensations within our own bodies, including feelings of hunger, satiation, thirst, heat and cold, and needing the toilet. Problems with this internal sensory system can mean that children do not recognise when they are hungry or thirsty, or when they have had enough to eat or drink. Children may feel sensations such as hunger, or fullness, but incorrectly interpret what these mean and so continue in discomfort, not able to recognise the correct solution. If children are distracted by uncomfortable bodily sensations that they cannot solve themselves, they will not be focusing on their learning, and their stress levels are likely to rise. Sensory difficulties can also be a factor in picky eating, as some textures might evoke a strong negative reaction, and a child may refuse to eat touching foods, especially if a food that is supposed to be crunchy or crispy has been made soggy by touching a wet food. If a child appears to have difficulties moving food round in their mouth, chewing or swallowing, sensory or motor difficulties may be the root cause.

One little girl I fostered was always asking for food and saying she was hungry, even a few minutes after eating an enormous meal. When I served up family meals, she would hover around, checking that she would be getting some of everything. I started serving her food first and got her a special plate that we used for every meal so that she could easily see what she was getting as I served.

She could not leave a meal unfinished or ever say she had had enough. Once, while we were on holiday, our evening meal was very late, and she ate it so fast that she was immediately sick right on to her plate. Another time I caught her eating other people's leftovers out of our kitchen bin.

For many people, food has an emotional element which is rooted in experiences of our early infancy when feeding was ideally a time of warmth, comfort and bonding with our primary caregiver. We talk about 'comfort eating' and 'comfort foods'. Children may also turn to food as a source of potential comfort, or as something to bring them pleasure and internal satisfaction when their lives are difficult. Children who have been regularly bribed with food, or had food withheld from them as a punishment, may have a particularly strong emotional connection with food.

Behaviour in the dining hall can also be a cause for concern. In common with other 'outside spaces', this can be an area with reduced supervision and an excess of sensory input, including increased noise and movement, and a mix of strong smells. Basic table manners, such as sitting at the table, using cutlery, eating at an appropriate speed, and serving an appropriate amount of shared food may simply be skills that a child hasn't previously been introduced to.

Approaches to try

- Ensure that opportunities to eat and drink are included on any visual timetable. Some children will need to be reassured that these times are coming, and others will need the visual prompt to remind them to have a drink or a snack.

- Try to avoid situations where there is a spread of food for children to help themselves from, such as a class party or food-tasting as part of a project. Where possible, portion the food in advance.

- If children are bringing in food to share, like pieces of birthday cake, make sure you, as the teacher, have control over where it is stored, and when and how it will be distributed. Ensure that this is incorporated onto children's daily planners or visual timetables. If possible, get it out of the way early in the day so it is not a continuing distraction.

- Frequent snacks regularly timetabled throughout the day can relieve craving for sugary food, and reduce anxiety around when food will next be available.

- Supervise the child closely at lunchtimes, especially if they are choosing food from counters in the dining room, so that they can be guided as to how to make a selection and what constitutes an appropriate portion size.

- Ensure that lunchtime supervisors responsible for serving food are aware of children who may need extra guidance and support. It is better for children to take a little now, but know that they will be allowed back for second helpings if they need more later.

- Provide the child with pictures, to scale, of appropriate portion sizes of various foods.

- Take the opportunity to discuss feelings around food when studying the human digestive system, for instance, by talking about portion size in relation to the size of an average human stomach, or exploring the different ways our body tells us that we are hungry or full.

- Predictability and timing of meals and snacks can be very important, so try to avoid keeping a child in at break or lunchtime so that they miss their snack or are late for their lunch. If the child is anxious, and focusing on when they will get their food, they will not be listening to what you are saying, or concentrating on their extra work anyway.

- Communicate with parents and carers about any strategies they use to support their child. This might include packing lunch and snack items in separate, labelled containers, or keeping a daily log of drinks.

- Avoid using food as a reward or punishment.

Toilet troubles

Dealing with problems relating to school toilets can be a drain on staff resources, whether the issue is children repeatedly asking to go during lesson times, children not going when they perhaps should have done, or groups congregating there during break times. Added to the disruption that is caused to lessons when children frequently excuse themselves to use the toilet, it is not unheard of for students to plan to meet up in the toilets at a pre-arranged time as part of a group escape strategy, with all the obvious risks that entails. School policies have to walk a delicate balance between ensuring children have the dignity of being able to attend to their most basic needs appropriately, while maintaining the focus on learning during lessons, and ensuring that toilets don't become hotspots of illicit activity.

Children with a history of trauma may have particular additional needs around toileting. Gaps in their development may mean that they arrive at school behind their peers in terms of toilet training, or lacking the manual dexterity to manage their own buttons and zips, especially if they are in a hurry because of urgent need. As we have seen when considering food issues, a poorly developed sense of interoception may mean that children are unaware of when they need the toilet, and can result in them wetting and soiling themselves. Both sensory difficulties, and executive functioning difficulties, can lead to a child not thinking to use the toilet at break time, but then having an urgent need five minutes after the lesson has started, either because they didn't realise they needed the toilet, or because they ran out of time. This is a particular difficulty for children who take longer than others to pack up their belongings, to move around the school, or to find the next place they are supposed to be.

Other children may be aware of their need, but find themselves unable to express that need. For children whose attachment difficulties mean that they are avoidant, and use invisibility as a shield, asking to go to the toilet in front of the whole class may be a step too far. This can be exacerbated once puberty hits, and young girls have menstruation to deal with. Periods can also be difficult to manage for girls with developmental delay who may lack the necessary skills to predict their needs, and plan ahead.

> Our daughter experienced internet bullying, with photos taken by other pupils within school posted on social media. She was so scared at one point in high school...that she would often wet herself and be in wet clothes all day, even though she had spare clothes. She had disassociated herself, she was so stressed.

Some children wet or soil themselves at school, and seem unaware, or unconcerned. This behaviour may be rooted in neglect if children have been used to being dirty and smelly, or were frequently left in soiled nappies, so that they do not have any sense of revulsion to being soiled, or it could be a sign that a child has dissociated. Children may also wet or soil if they have been holding on in order to avoid asking to use the toilet, or so that they can continue their current activity. Unfortunately, toilets can sometimes be dirty and smelly, or become areas where children congregate and hidden bullying can take place, which may be a factor in some children avoiding visiting them outside of lesson times. However, some medical conditions can be exacerbated if children avoid, or have limited access to, toilets at school, and avoiding drink during the day in order to minimise need for the toilet is not likely to be conducive to children being in an optimal state to learn. While it can be frustrating and disruptive to have children visiting the toilet during lesson time, there are a number of legitimate reasons why a child might simply have been unable to attend to their own needs during the break time. Involving children in creating a whole-school toilet policy may go some way to assuaging staff concerns about unrestricted access to toilet facilities, while indicating to children that their dignity and welfare is important to the school.

Approaches to try

- Audit the toilet facilities at school, and gather children's views in order to identify any problems or concerns.

- Formulate a whole-school policy that takes account of the dignity, welfare and safety of children, while balancing the need for the school to have some oversight of use of toilet facilities. The Enuresis Resource and Information Centre (ERIC), has a sample school toilet policy freely available on their website (www.eric.org.uk).

- As children are being dismissed for break times or lunchtime, remind them that this is a good time to visit the toilet. Similarly, a few minutes before the end of lunchtime, supervisors can encourage children to visit the toilet before lessons begin.

- Incorporate visits to the toilet as part of a child's visual or written timetable.

- If you suspect that a child is holding on because they don't want to leave their activity, reassure them that you will keep their activity safe until they return.

- Wetting and soiling can be really frustrating for the adults involved. Keep your tone even and your words neutral in order to avoid exacerbating a child's shame.

- Children with sensory issues may not know the answer to the question, 'Do you need the toilet?' A more direct approach might work better. For instance, 'I can see you are jiggling around. It's time to go to the toilet now.'

- If expressing their needs is a problem, provide the child with a non-verbal means of indicating that they need to use the toilet.

Chapter 12

TESTING TIMES

In this chapter:

Homework and revision

Coursework and timed work

Coping with tests and exams

In a culture where schools are increasingly judged according to their students' achievements in statutory examinations, there is an understandable focus on raising attainment and promoting academic excellence, yet the achievement of vulnerable groups of children falls consistently behind that of their peers. In England, only 25 per cent of looked-after children, and 31 per cent of previously looked-after children achieved the expected standard at Key Stage 2 in 2016, compared to 53 per cent of their peers (DfE 2016). At GCSE level, 2016 figures from the Department of Education show that while 53 per cent of all children achieved five good grades (including English and Maths), fewer than 14 per cent of looked-after children, and just a quarter of previously looked-after children, achieved the same standard (DfE 2017a). The new measures of attainment introduced in 2017 show that the gap remains significant, with these cohorts' attainment levels being much lower than their peers in every measure (DfE 2018a; Dfe 2018b).

Why the discrepancy? Is it just that children who are, or who have been, in care are pre-destined to fall behind and fail at school? Research by the organisation Become suggests that negative stereotypes about children in care do exist in schools. Their *Teachers Who Care* report (Become 2018) found that three-quarters of teachers had heard colleagues express the view that children in care are less likely to succeed in life, and 70 per cent had heard the view the children in care are 'problem children'. Perhaps most worryingly, nearly half of respondents had heard colleagues generalise that children in care are less academically able than their peers. The report concludes that teachers 'need to be supportive and understanding, while also being ambitious for looked after children, and seeing that they have inherent potential equal to their peers'. The attainment statistics for looked-after and previously looked-after children must be seen not as an indication that there is no hope of success, but as a motivation to raise expectations and redress the balance for children whose lives have been affected by trauma, loss and serious disruption through no fault of their own, and often before they even had their first day at school. Low expectations must not allow us to be satisfied that an individual care-experienced child bucked the trend to achieve a few good grades in statutory examinations if, with additional support, they could have got top grades. Not all children have an equal start in life, but all must have an equal chance in school.

> My son is a very compliant young man who doesn't cause disruption in class and is on course at the moment to achieve five good GCSEs. Therefore he is simply not a priority for an over-stretched SEN [Special Educational Needs] department. We are trying to get the school to acknowledge that with the correct support for his anxiety and sensory processing difficulties he could probably be doing far better.

Throughout this book, a case has been made for the possibility of a brighter educational future for children who have experienced trauma, abuse, neglect, loss, family disruption and other adverse childhood experiences. The impact of these cannot be ignored, but neither are children's outcomes set in stone. We can, and should, have high expectations for all children. As trauma-informed teachers, we do not seek to 'make excuses for bad behaviour', nor to lower expectations in terms of attainment, but rather to accept that understanding the root causes of challenging behaviour and poor attainment, and addressing those, will be more effective in the long term than punishing or excluding without understanding. If we genuinely have high expectations for a child, and truly wish to see them achieve and succeed, then we must not give up on them if they don't respond to our systems and protocols in the desired way. We, as the adults, must find a better way.

Children with developmental trauma need reasonable adjustments and extra support if they are to be expected to reach the same goals as other children. If we don't punish a child with dyslexia for struggling to read, or punish a child in a wheelchair for not running the cross-country, we should not punish a child with sensory processing difficulties for reacting negatively to overwhelming sensory information, or a child with weak executive functioning skills who forgets their pencil. Instead, as teachers, we seek to understand the underlying problem, and find and implement strategies to overcome it or, if it is not possible to overcome it, to manage it through reasonable adjustments.

Raising attainment in children who have experienced trauma and adverse childhood experiences begins with a whole-school commitment to understanding the impact of those experiences which filters down into every classroom, every corridor and every conversation. There are resources and interventions that can be used to support this, but approaching a struggling child with empathy and curiosity costs nothing. If we truly want to redress the balance for some of our most vulnerable children, then recognising and adjusting for their underlying challenges and difficulties is the first step. When children are in the classroom, rather than excluded from it, when they feel safe, and when their basic needs are catered for, then they will be ready and able to learn to their potential. Until a child reaches this point, interventions designed to support progress in, say, numeracy or literacy are unlikely to be as effective as they could be. Once they are ready, then, as a teacher, you probably already know the resources and pedagogical approaches that will work to best effect in your classroom.

> There's a huge discrepancy between my child's academic and emotional ability, which puts high demand and expectation on her head that she simply cannot manage.

Trauma-informed practice is not an optional extra; it is a necessary pre-cursor to genuine inclusion for all children. There are times in every child's life when parents and carers have to walk a fine line between managing their child's emotional needs and mental health, and encouraging them with their school work. During times of bereavement, family breakdown or crisis, or physical or mental ill-health, school work may slide, and compassionate, responsive strategies may be needed to support an individual child. When a school moves towards a trauma-informed approach, it not only benefits those with a background of complex or prolonged trauma, but also those who may be experiencing current stressful or traumatic situations. If we fail to recognise the impact of traumatic experiences of all types on the abilities of children to learn and to make progress, then we are setting them up to fail.

Homework and revision

These two thorny issues are grouped together because they both move the onus of responsibility for learning from school into the home environment and, as such, can easily become a source of conflict between families and schools.

> Homework is a huge stress factor in our home. My son is exhausted at the end of the school day with the academic, emotional and social demands of school. Homework tips him over the edge and meltdowns are frequent. He requires constant supervision and support to complete homework.

Children who are carrying the additional burden of sensory processing difficulties, hyper-vigilance, anxiety, communication difficulties, delayed physical development and raised cortisol levels, are working much harder to manage a normal school day than some of their peers are. Once they arrive home at the end of the day, they may be exhausted, and no longer able to maintain the coping strategies that have enabled them to survive the day, leading to meltdowns and challenging behaviour, even in a child who appears calm and compliant at school.

Homework blurs the dividing line between school and home. It puts the parent or carer into the position of assistant teacher, which can place a strain on a developing attachment relationship and add complication to already difficult transitions between school and home. If the child has weak executive functioning skills, then even arriving home with the right equipment can be a challenge, never mind remembering what the homework entails and how to complete it. Too often, parents and carers have to provide continuous supervision if any homework is to be completed, which is not always possible if they have work or other caring responsibilities. Exhausted children, or those with additional learning needs, will take longer to complete homework, so school work then eats into family time, playtime and activity time.

> My child absolutely doesn't have an equal chance compared to his peers. They've had 'x' years to form as a family; we adopted him when he was in Reception. The homework expectations are more manageable when you have a securely attached child. When you're still forming the attachment and every homework negotiation is viewed as a potential for rejection – wow!

The expectation that parents and carers will take responsibility for ensuring that children's homework is completed to a reasonable standard and within a certain time frame can prove unrealistic for many families. Some children live in chaotic homes where parents are not able or available to support homework, or where there is no calm or quiet space to complete it. Others have caring duties, and may even be caring for the adults who are supposed to be helping them with homework. Children of working parents may have to wait to start their homework until after their parents come home from work, squeezing it all into the twilight hour between teatime and bedtime when they are least likely to be up for the challenge. Some children with additional needs will also need to fit in theraplay activities, a sensory integration programme, or other therapeutic interventions during this time.

As children grow older, it might be expected that they will increasingly be able to complete their homework and revision independently, but for children with additional needs, including those rooted in trauma, this independence may come a lot later, if at all. For instance, it is widely expected that children will be able to access the internet at home in order to complete work. While 98 per cent of households with children do have internet access at home (ONS, 2017), safety on the internet is a concern for parents and carers, especially where children and young people are particularly vulnerable, lack the ability to properly assess risks, or may search for or be found by birth family members who may pose a risk to them. In fact, ThinkUknow, Child Exploitation and Online Protection's (CEOP) internet safety education programme, includes specific advice and information for adoptive parents and foster carers because this additional risk is considered so significant. In these circumstances, it is likely that parents and carers will need to closely supervise any internet activity, including homework tasks, research and revision online.

Revision for exams and tests is also an area where a growing independence might be expected to play a part. In reality, many children of 15 or 16 years old will need support to devise a sensible revision timetable and stick to it, as well as to develop the skills needed for effective revision.

For children with a background of trauma, all the challenges involved in homework apply equally to revision at home. Weak executive functioning skills make creating and sticking to a revision plan particularly difficult, and exhaustion from managing a long school day means that there is little reserve left over for effective revision at home in the evenings. The additional stress of looming exams may mean that children are on a hair trigger, and attempts by parents or carers to encourage them to revise in the evenings and at weekends can provoke meltdowns and aggressive behaviour.

Approaches to try

- Ensure that expectations around homework are commensurate not just with a child's chronological age and abilities, but also with their emotional and developmental age.

- Work with parents and carers to establish whether the child is capable of completing the homework task within a reasonable time frame. If an activity that is intended to take 20 minutes is actually taking a child over an hour to complete, then adjustments need to be made. Even if a child can work within the time frame in school, tiredness, distractions, hunger and other factors can mean they work much more slowly at home.

- Provide extra support to ensure that the child knows what is expected of them and has all the equipment they will need.

- Ensure that the child has the homework written down for them, on a printed sheet for example. Do not rely on children of any age to remember, or even to make their own accurate record of the set task in a homework diary.

- Where possible, allow parents to suggest creative alternatives to homework tasks that are less likely to cause tension and resistance, for example, watching a documentary on the subject, playing a word or number game, or taking a guided nature walk.

- Discuss the possibility of making use of the schools before- and after-school clubs with the childs parents or carers.

- Provide extra revision clubs and groups during exam season for children who face particular challenges in completing revision independently whether because of special educational needs, the impact of early trauma, or current adverse experiences.

- Be explicit about teaching various methods for revision, including those that draw on children's particular strengths and compensate for difficulties.

- Be aware that there may be times in a child's life when completing homework takes a second place. For looked-after and previously looked-after children, the importance of maintaining a stable placement or home life must take priority. If a foster care placement, or an adoptive family is in danger of disruption, then anything that raises the risk of disruption must be minimised in its impact. There will be time in the future for a child to catch up on missed education, but the effects on a child of multiple care placements, or the breakdown of an adoptive family, are devastating and lifelong.

Coursework and timed work

Both longer-term coursework projects, and shorter, timed pieces of work, require children to use quite sophisticated planning and time-management skills. Poor executive functioning skills can be a feature of Foetal Alcohol Spectrum Disorder (FASD) conditions and developmental trauma, meaning that children who would otherwise perhaps be capable of completing the task are hampered by inability to organise themselves, structure their work and plan their approach and their timing. The pressure of a ticking timer, or the rapidly moving hands of a clock may be a powerful motivator for some children, but for those whose anxiety levels are already high, and whose stress-management skills may be affected by trauma, such pressure can overwhelm logical, rational thinking, leading to a fight–flight–freeze response.

Children with attachment difficulties, and especially with Reactive Attachment Disorder, typically have a very low and negative view of themselves. Their ability to persist and persevere when faced with tasks which appear difficult may be extremely poor, so that lengthy, multi-faceted coursework projects, or a vital piece of timed work on which a significant proportion of their final grade might depend, can seem insurmountable. This goes beyond low self-esteem, or the kind of self-doubt that many experience from time to time. The feelings of being useless, worthless and no good are deeply entrenched, learned from infancy, and are not easily overcome, even when previous successes are pointed out. Many children with attachment difficulties and disorders achieve below their potential partly because they simply cannot believe the extent of their own potential, and give up on themselves. We might all fear failure from time to time, but children with a negative internal view of themselves caused by attachment disorders don't just fear failure, they anticipate it as a certainty, and may prefer to resist engaging in tasks in order to avoid what they imagine will be the certain shame and humiliation that will follow.

> The head of sixth form is brilliant and spends much time talking to her and trying to help her overcome her self-esteem issues, but she often fails to attend classes even when in school and this is affecting her progress. Although she is very talented at Art, she cannot accept that, and cannot produce the amount of work required to achieve the grade she should at A-level. Her other subject is Philosophy and again, she avoids the work, and cannot concentrate or organise herself to attain her potential.

Approaches to try

- Think of a child with weak executive functioning skills as having a specific learning difficulty. Interventions and support should be designed to enable that child to achieve their potential as if that specific difficulty did not exist. Support might include working with the child to formulate a plan for completing longer coursework projects in short, timed stages, with each step in each stage clearly defined.

- Practise timed work, using scaffolding (such as writing frames) to help the child organise their thoughts and get them down on paper.

- Encourage the child to use post-it notes or other visual methods to plan essays.

- Use colour to highlight important information on questions and task descriptions.

- Be aware that behaviours such as 'giving up', 'not trying' or 'messing around' may be masking feelings of vulnerability.

- Work with the child to build up a 'strengths profile' highlighting areas where they can succeed and have succeeded, and especially noting the skills they used to overcome their difficulties. Refer to this regularly, especially when introducing a new activity or task. Identify areas of weakness as well, and formulate plans to improve or overcome these little by little.

- Break down the steps required for timed pieces of work, indicating what constitutes a reasonable amount of time to spend on each step.

- Allow the child extra time to complete timed work. Where possible, try setting no time limit. A child who becomes anxious under time pressure may find that they can complete the work within the required time frame if the source of their anxiety is removed.

- Provide choices. For instance, if students need to complete six questions, set ten and ask the students to choose six. Having more control over the work they do could support some students to complete the six questions, rather than giving up before doing the first one.

Coping with tests and exams

For most children, the statutory exams they take towards the end of the secondary phase of their education will feel like the final say on their attainment, but the stress and pressure of exam season, coupled with the turbulence of adolescence can make this an especially difficult time for young people who have experienced trauma. Some adopted and looked-after children will seek to create, or develop, relationships with their birth families during their teens, and others may be found unexpectedly by birth relatives on social media, bringing an added dimension of emotional strain into their lives that other children do not have to deal with. Care-experienced teens are often facing all the challenges of their peers, plus many more associated with their history and current situation. Even children who have benefited from many years of trauma-informed support in school may need extra help as final exams loom, in addition to the support they may attract because of any recognised special educational needs.

There is pressure on every child surrounding any test or exam perceived as 'high-stakes'. This is then coupled with the reality that many of the coping strategies that might enable a child to manage well enough in the classroom will not be appropriate during a formal examination. A child cannot take a sensory break, for instance, in a room where others are sitting silently working on their tests. The impact of the change in routine associated with exam time should also not be under-estimated. Children may be on study leave, arriving at school at different times than usual, going to different rooms, and being supervised by staff they have little previous relationship with. For a child who struggles with transitions and change, walking into a previously familiar environment, and finding everything changed – displays removed, tables and chairs rearranged – is disorientating and unsettling, and then we expect them to sit still for an hour or two and produce the best work of their lives.

> Anxiety around tests and timed work is an issue for both of our adopted children. They feel shame and a negative sense of self when they get things wrong in school. This tends to lead to a fog descending and an inability to engage, problem solve and persevere.

Exam time, whether in primary or secondary school, can be the moment when problems that have been simmering under the surface for years suddenly come to the fore. Children who have previously seemed to cope well, and appeared 'fine', may break down completely under the additional strain. Minds may become blank, coping mechanisms may fail, and a fight–flight–freeze stage can be quickly reached. For some, this may mean a poor performance on the day, with results significantly below expectations. For others it may mean bolting out of the exam hall within minutes of the start and blowing their chances altogether. Identifying children who are likely to find exam time particularly challenging, and implementing strategies to support them well ahead of their exams starting, may mean the difference between them achieving their potential, or walking away with nothing.

Approaches to try

- Ensure that children are familiar with the look and feel of the room where they will be sitting their exams ahead of time. Practise being in there and completing low-stakes work in there (do not view mock exams as this practice opportunity).

- Go through the routines associated with sitting exams several times so that they feel familiar. For instance, practise lining up outside the room, finding desks, sorting equipment, reading the examination rubric, and go through arrangements for visiting the toilet. Be very explicit during these rehearsals about what type of help children may or may not ask for during the exam.

- Use visual schedules and cue cards instead of lengthy verbal instructions.

- Consider assessing children for extra time in the exam, if anxiety, stress, executive functioning difficulties or other challenges are likely to cause difficulties.

- Ensure that key adults are available during the examination periods, especially at the beginning of each exam.

- Arrange for the child to sit their exams in a separate room where they can take movement and sensory breaks if necessary.

- Study leave can be counter-productive if children are resistant to parental input, or are alone for much of the day while parents or carers work, and struggle to plan and organise revision during this time. Consider running revision classes in school instead of study leave for children who face particular challenges.

- In preparation for exams, and during the examination period, ensure that expectations are appropriate, and guidance includes children of all attainment levels. It can be de-motivating for children to repeatedly hear that employers and colleges expect the highest grades when experience has taught them that they are unlikely to achieve these grades. Make the message about doing their best, rather than being the best.

THE DE FERRERS ACADEMY

Towards more effective approaches to raising attainment

Four years ago, The de Ferrers Academy embarked on a project known as RADY (Raising Attainment of Disadvantaged Youngsters) in conjunction with Challenging Education [UK-based education consultants]. The project aims to reduce the attainment gap experienced by disadvantaged children, and those entitled to Pupil

Premium in particular, by addressing gaps in their learning which may have been caused by missing out on essential stages of early development, the impact of trauma, or gaps in their early education.

RADY begins by raising expectations for the Pupil Premium cohort at Year 7. Reported Key Stage 2 SATs[1] results are adjusted to take account of the impact of disadvantage, and to make them more in line with target-setting for other members of the year group. As a result, many children will enter Year 7 in a higher set and with higher targets than their original SATs results might have suggested. Initially, these children may appear to be working below their targets due to this uplift, and this triggers specific, targeted interventions to address gaps in their learning during Key Stage 3, and support them to work to their higher targets.

The first RADY cohort is yet to take GCSE[2] exams, but early results indicate that the attainment gap is being closed. During Year 7, this first cohort, the class of 2020, achieved a progress score of 5.51 points over the year in Maths, compared to an average progress score of 4.9 for the whole year group. This was a huge increase on the progress score of the previous year's cohort of disadvantaged students, which was just 3.44. Achievement in English was similarly improved, with disadvantaged students gaining 4.58, while their peers gained 3.78 over the year. When children's future targets are not determined by past performance which may be skewed by factors outside of their control, the attainment gap really can be narrowed. De Ferrers is optimistic that the cohort's GCSE results will reflect this enhanced progress.

However, interventions to support disadvantaged students at de Ferrers do not begin and end with target-setting. Sarah Glover, Groups Achievement Leader, heads up the RADY project. She explains that the school is increasingly aware of the need to focus on understanding behaviour and supporting children with their mental health and social skills. She acknowledges that, 'It is especially apparent that this is needed for our looked-after and adopted students.'

The school has invested in attachment training for all staff members, which Sarah describes as the most powerful tool they have used.

---

1   Standard attainment tests taken by English children in their final year of primary school (aged 11).

2   General Certificate of Secondary Education – examinations taken by English, Welsh and Northern Irish students at around age 16.

Subsequently, although the school's behavioural policy is, in Sarah's own words, 'rigid', all staff have been engaged in approaches designed to effectively support all children to meet behavioural expectations, and to sensitively manage difficulties, making reasonable adjustments where necessary.

Teachers establish the atmosphere of the classroom for each lesson by greeting each student as they enter, and engaging them in activities immediately. Every lesson is a fresh start, with no grudges held over from previous incidents. Minor misdemeanours are dealt with, as far as possible, through low-key, even non-verbal means and, when more serious behavioural challenges arise, there are safe areas and dedicated mentors on hand across all three sites of this 2000-pupil school.

A great deal of thought is given to classroom layout and seating arrangements. While it is tempting to seat the more challenging students right under the teacher's nose, children who have experienced trauma prioritise feeling safe when they are choosing where to sit, and allowing them to take a seat against a wall, for instance, might avert a crisis. Once the task is set, members of staff will go immediately to RADY students to check that they have understood what is expected of them, and help to break it down into manageable steps if they seem overwhelmed or unsure where to start.

Training has also supported staff members to be more aware of potential triggers in the curriculum. Teachers of Values and Religious Studies will often talk to students in advance of certain topics, and when *The Woman in Black* [a ghost story] was a trigger for a particular looked-after student recently, the English teacher recognised this, and changed the text for the whole class.

Effective communications form the foundation for the success of the school's approach to supporting disadvantaged children. Every teacher should know who the Pupil Premium students in their classroom are, as well as those who are gifted and talented, or who have SEND, or English as an additional language. Links between the RADY project leader and the SEND department ensure that individual student passports state reasonable adjustments that need to be made for specific children. The Virtual School[3] also has a key role to play,

---

3   An English local authority department with responsibility for overseeing the education of looked-after and previously looked-after children in their area.

and the school works closely with the Virtual School Head. Finally, and perhaps most importantly, communications between home and school are frequent and responsive. Handwritten praise postcards provide a record of children's achievements and successes, and Learning Mentors build relationships with parents and carers as well as with students.

Sarah states honestly that this project has not all been plain sailing, and some resistance was experienced in the early days. However, as she says, 'this lessened as the students became more engaged and attainment started to gradually equalise in some groups'. Once members of staff saw that the strategies were working, enthusiasm for the project increased. However, although progress has been made, de Ferrers is not planning to rest on its collective laurels. Alternative provision is being developed, including the Forest School [an outdoor play and learning facility], work placements and flexible timetabling, and the RADY team is looking at more effective ways of communicating individual students' needs with all members of staff. Recent training in the Boxall Profile [an assessment tool for social, emotional and behavioural difficulties in children] will generate new strategies to support students at risk of exclusion.

Making school-wide changes is not an easy task in a secondary school of this size, with a sixth form and three campuses, but the results of the project speak for themselves, creating a tide of optimism about the possibilities for disadvantaged students which is difficult to ignore.

Chapter 13

SECONDARY TRAUMA IS REAL

Too often, advice for parents and carers of traumatised children seems to give the impression that the adults are equivalent to infinite sponges, able to continually absorb anything the children throw at them, sometimes literally, with no adverse effects on their own physical or mental wellbeing. This is obviously not realistic, either for parents, or teachers, or any other professional working with people who have experienced trauma.

The reality is that supporting a child who has experienced trauma, and who displays the impact of that trauma in their daily interactions, takes its toll on those who care for them. A truly trauma-informed school needs to be concerned about not only the impact of trauma on the children passing through its doors, but also the impact of caring for and working with those children on all the adults involved. Traumatised children will sometimes display extremely challenging behaviours, or engage in attachment-seeking strategies to such an extent that they become an emotional drain on those around them, or disclose distressing information that haunts the dreams of those who hear it. Children can pinpoint adult vulnerabilities with frightening accuracy, make adults feel de-skilled, helpless and confused, and push them to their emotional limits. Sometimes the words and actions of a hurt child can seem very personally directed against the very staff member who has made a commitment to nurture and care for them. It is terribly sad that those children who most desperately need the security of relationships are often least equipped to develop and maintain them.

Whether your school is trauma-informed or not, you will most likely encounter children who have lived through trauma, and experience the secondary impact of that as you work with and alongside them each day. While trauma-informed practices can make an enormous positive difference to the way traumatised children manage in school, the reality is that coping with the effects of others' trauma can be draining and have lasting impacts on teachers' emotional and physical wellbeing. A senior leadership team that is moving towards a trauma-informed approach must take account not only of the traumatised children, but also of the adults who work with them. No teacher should ever be left to cope unsupported with a child who manifests the devastating and sometimes destructive consequences of trauma in their classroom. This means top-down recognition of the impact of coping with the effects of others' trauma on staff members, and robust support systems made available to all.

Educators who work regularly with traumatised children can sometimes develop their own symptoms of traumatic stress, often called secondary trauma, secondary traumatic stress or, sometimes, vicarious trauma. This can be exacerbated if the adult has personal experience of similar traumatic events, is currently managing the impact of their own trauma, is hearing traumatic stories directly from a child, feels isolated and unsupported, or is locked in a cycle of caring for others without caring for themselves.

Anybody can be at risk of secondary trauma. It is not a sign of weakness, or failure to cope, or a result of poor practice. It can manifest as low mood, fatigue, feeling hopeless or overwhelmed, lack of concentration, sleep disturbance, guilt, emotional unavailability, hair trigger reactions, aggression, feeling on edge and anxious, feeling numb – in short, many of the same symptoms exhibited by the traumatised children themselves.

Self-care certainly has a role to play in protecting against, and mitigating the effects of, secondary trauma. Adults are likely to be more resilient if they are sleeping enough, eating healthily, exercising and finding time to engage in leisure activities and to spend with friends and family. However, the responsibility for managing secondary trauma should not fall on the individual teacher alone. Schools are complex communities, and everybody needs to be involved in creating a safe environment for both adults and children, as everybody is affected when this does not happen.

Senior leaders can begin by recognising the reality of secondary trauma in a completely non-judgemental way. When secondary trauma makes a staff member feel isolated and overwhelmed, lack of support from the senior leadership team will only exacerbate this. It is important that school leaders acknowledge that not only are staff members doing a great job, but they are also doing a difficult job, and that those who need support because of secondary trauma are not struggling with personal weakness, but experiencing the understandable effects of a very challenging situation. A responsive leadership will normalise conversations about staff wellbeing, and ensure that support is available to all staff at all times, rather than responding reactively to a crisis.

School policies need to be pro-active in ensuring that staff members are able to practise appropriate levels of self-care. Drained and exhausted teachers who have spent their evenings marking, planning and working for weeks on end are unlikely to bring the level of resilience they need to the classroom to support challenging and traumatised children. During the school day, adults need the opportunity to fulfil their most basic needs such as drinking and eating and using the toilet, just as much as children do. If the demands of work exceed a person's ability to cope, then the risk of developing secondary trauma is increased. Investment in the wellbeing of school staff is never wasted.

School leaders can also be instrumental in ensuring that educators are trained and resourced to best support the children in their classes. If a child with Foetal Alcohol Spectrum Disorder (FASD), for instance, is to be in a teacher's class next year, then that teacher, and all other adults who work in the classroom, will need appropriate and up-to-date training on the condition and its implications, and time to consider how to apply this knowledge in the classroom setting. It is incredibly stressful for a teacher to be confronted daily with a child with complex difficulties, without the skills and resources to effectively support that child. If classroom staff feel that additional resources, or external professional expertise is required, then their requests should be supported, not only as a means to helping the child, but also as a means to supporting the adults in their challenging role.

Staff will sometimes need a place to share how they are feeling, without being judged, so peer-to-peer support, perhaps with a trained facilitator, can be invaluable, especially for those key adults, 1-1 workers and class teachers who spend the most time with traumatised children. Regular meetings will be arranged between those staff members to support the child's development and progress, but time dedicated to supporting the adults who are working with the child is also important and should not be viewed as an optional extra. Sharing experiences, strategies and stories can build hope and optimism when the present situation seems relentlessly difficult. Just as traumatised children benefit from secure, nurturing relationships, so do staff members experiencing secondary trauma. A strong, supportive staff community can provide a safe foundation for each of its members, so consider building in simple, optional shared activities such as short walks at lunchtime.

Events when the whole staff comes together can be opportunities to build community and relationships, acknowledge the outstanding work that staff members are involved in, and outline the ways in which every adult can be supported within the school community. It is unfortunately all too easy to fall into a mindset of negativity, especially as a teacher's job is never really done – there is always another goal ahead. Whole staff training days can be a chance to reset this mindset, and reflect positively on what has already been achieved, and what realistically can be achieved in the coming term.

Many of us will have embarked on a career in education with ideas of influencing future generations, passing on a love of learning, and perhaps being the inspirational figure in the life of a young person that one of our teachers was to us. Maybe a few years in the classroom will re-shape our idealism somewhat, but the truth is that educators do have an enormous impact on the children they teach. Those children and young people may not remember everything we said, or everything we taught them, but they will remember who we were. For children whose life experiences so far have been fraught with difficulty and adversity, a safe, secure and nurturing school can be transformative, and it is well-supported, highly skilled educators who will be at the heart of that transformation.

My son's new school is understanding, loving, kind and adopts an amazing approach to wellbeing. He is like a new boy. It can work!

References

Adoption UK (November 2017) *Schools and Exclusions Report.* Available at www.adoptionuk. org/Handlers/Download.ashx?IDMF=e6616ae3-7b0a-449c-b037-070a92428495) (accessed 22/1/2019).

Adoption UK (June 2018) *Bridging the Gap: Giving Adopted and all Traumatised Children an Equal Chance in School.* Available at www.adoptionuk.org/Handlers/Download. ashx?IDMF=e460b99a-4ebb-4348-bd23-64a50d747901 (accessed 22/1/2019).

Ainsworth, M.D.S. and Bell, S.M. (1970) 'Attachment, exploration, and separation: Illustrated by the behavior of one-year-olds in a strange situation.' *Child Development, 41,* 49–67.

American Psychiatric Association. (2013). *Diagnostic and statistical manual of mental disorders (5th ed.).* Arlington, VA.

Andreassen, C. and West, J. (2007) 'Measuring socioemotional functioning in a national birth cohort study.' *Infant Mental Health Journal, 28,* 6, 627–646.

Aron, E. (2015) *The Highly Sensitive Child.* London: Thorsons.

Become (2018) *Teachers Who Care.* Available at www.becomecharity.org.uk/for-professionals/ resources/teachers-who-care (accessed 15/2/2019).

Belsky, J. and Fearon, R. (2002) 'Infant–mother attachment security, contextual risk, and early development: A moderational analysis.' *Development and Psychopathology, 14,* 361–387.

Bernier, A., Carlson, S.M., Deschanes, M. and Matte-Gagne, C. (2012) 'Social factors in the development of early executive functioning: A closer look at the caregiving environment.' *Developmental Science, 15,* 1, 12–24.

Bombèr, L.M. (2007) *Inside I'm Hurting.* Twickenham: Worth Publishing.

Bremness, A. and Polzin, W. (2014) 'Commentary: Developmental Trauma Disorder: A Missed Opportunity in DSM 5.' *Journal of the Canadian Academy of Child and Adolescent Psychiatry, 23,* 2, 142–145.

British Medical Association (BMA) (June 2007, updated February 2016) *Alcohol and Pregnancy: Preventing and Managing Fetal Alcohol Spectrum Disorders.* London: BMA.

Brooks, F. (2014) 'The link between pupil health and wellbeing and attainment.' London: Public Health England.

de Thierry, B. (2017) *The Simple Guide to Child Trauma: What It Is and How To Help.* London: Jessica Kingsley Publishers.

Department for Education (2016) *National curriculum assessments at key stage 2 in England, 2016 (provisional).* SFR 39/2016.

Department for Education (2017a) *Outcomes for children looked after by local authorities in England, 31 March 2016: additional tables.* SFR 12/2017.

Department for Education (2017b) *Revised GCSE and equivalent results in England, 2015 to 2016.* SFR 03/2017.

Department for Education (2018a) *Revised GCSE and equivalent results in England, 2016 to 2017.* SFR 01/2018.

Department for Education (2018b) *Outcomes for children looked after by local authorities in England.* SFR 20/2018.

Department for Education and Department of Health (2015) *Special Educational Needs and Disability Code of Practice: 0 to 25 Years.* DFE-00205-2013. London: HMSO.

Dix, P. (2017) *When the Adults Change, Everything Changes.* Carmarthen: Independent Thinking Press.

Fearon, R.P., Bakermans-Kranenburg, M., van Ijzendoorn, M.H., Lapsley, A. and Roisman, G.I. (2010) 'The significance of insecure attachment and disorganization in the development of children's externalising behaviour: A meta-analytic study.' *Child Development, 81,* 2, 435–456.

Felitti, V.J., Anda, R.F., Nordenberg, D., Williamson, D.F., *et al.* (1998) 'Relationship of childhood abuse and household dysfunction to many of the leading causes of death in adults.' *American Journal of Preventative Medicine, 14,* 245–258.

Fryer, R.G. (2018) 'The "Pupil" Factory: Specialization and the Production of Human Capital in Schools.' *American Economic Review, 108,* 3, 616–656.

Gerhardt, S. (2014) *Why Love Matters.* London: Routledge.

Gonzalez, A. (2013) 'The impact of childhood maltreatment on biological systems: Implications for clinical interventions.' *Paediatrics Child Health, 18,* 8, 415–418.

Gore-Langton, E. and Boy, K. (2017) *Becoming an Adoption-Friendly School.* London: Jessica Kingsley Publishers.

Gregory, G., Reddy, V. and Young, C. (2015) 'Identifying children who are at risk of FASD in Peterborough: Working in a community clinic without access to gold standard diagnosis.' *Adoption & Fostering, 39,* 3, 225–234.

Guerri, C., Bazinet, A. and Riley, E.P. (2009) 'Foetal alcohol spectrum disorders and alterations in brain and behaviour.' *Alcohol and Alcoholism, 44,* 2, 108–114.

Gunnar, M.R. and Cheatham, C.L. (2003) 'Brain and behaviour interface: Stress and the developing brain.' *Infant Mental Health Journal, 24,* 3, 195–211.

Gutman, L.M. and Vorhaus, J. (2012) 'The impact of pupil behaviour and wellbeing on educational outcomes.' DFE-RR253. London: Department of Education.

Hill, A.J. and Jones, D.B. (2018) 'A teacher who knows me: The academic benefits of repeat student–teacher matches.' *Economics of Education Review, 64,* 1–12.

LeWinn, K.Z., Stroud, L.R., Molnar, B.E., Ware, J.H., Koenen, K.C. and Buka, S.L. (2009) 'Elevated maternal cortisol levels during pregnancy are associated with reduced childhood IQ.' *International Journal of Epidemiology, 38,* 6, 1700–1710.

Main, M. and Solomon, J. (1990) 'Procedures for identifying infants as disorganized/disoriented during the Ainsworth Strange Situation.' In M.T. Greenberg, D. Cicchetti and E.M. Cummings (eds) *Attachment in the Preschool Years.* Chicago, IL: University of Chicago Press.

Mattson, S.N. and Riley, E.P. (1998) 'A Review of the Neurobehavioral Deficits in Children with Fetal Alcohol Syndrome or Prenatal Exposure to Alcohol.' *Alcoholism: Clinical and Experimental Research, 22,* 2.

McCloud, C. and Messing, D. (2015) *Have You Filled a Bucket Today? A Guide to Daily Happiness for Kids.* Northville, MI: Ferne Press.

Moran, H.J. (2010) 'Clinical observations of the differences between children in the autism spectrum and those with attachment problems: The Coventry Grid.' *Good Autism Practice, 11,* 2, 46–59.

Naish, S. (2018) *The A–Z of Therapeutic Parenting.* London: Jessica Kingsley Publishers.

NHS Choices (2018) 'Complex PTSD.' Available at www.nhs.uk/conditions/post-traumatic-stress-disorder-ptsd/complex (accessed 15/2/2019).

NICE guideline [NG26] (November 2015) *Children's attachment: Attachment in children and young people who are adopted from care, in care or at high risk of going into care.* London: NICE.

Nikulina, V. and Widom, C.S. (2013) 'Child maltreatment and executive functioning in middle adulthood: A prospective examination.' *Neuropsychology, 27*, 4, July.

Office for National Statistics, 2017. *Internet access – households and individuals, Great Britain: 2017.* Available at https://www.ons.gov.uk/peoplepopulationandcommunity/householdcharacteristics/homeinternetandsocialmediausage/bulletins/internetaccesshouseholdsandindividuals/2017 (accessed 17/06/2018).

Owen, J.P., Marco, E.J., Desai, S., Fourie, E., *et al.* (2013) 'Abnormal white matter microstructure in children with sensory processing disorders.' *NeuroImage: Clinical, 2*, 844–853.

Perry, B.D. and The Child Trauma Academy. (2017) *What is NMT?* Presentation available online at https://childtrauma.org/wp-content/uploads/2018/01/CTA_NMT_Core-Slides_2018r.pdf (accessed 14/4/2019).

Rees, J. (2017) *Life Story Books for Adopted and Fostered Children.* London: Jessica Kingsley Publishers.

Siegel, D. (1999) *The Developing Mind: How Relationships and the Brain Interact to Shape Who We Are.* New York: Guilford Press.

Siegel, D. (2010) *Mindsight: The New Science of Personal Transformation.* Bantam.

Siegel, Daniel J. (2012) *The Developing Mind: How Relationships and the Brain Interact to Shape Who We Are.* Second edition. New York: The Guilford Press.

Supin, J. (2016) 'The Long Shadow: Bruce Perry on the lingering effects of childhood trauma.' *The Sun*, November. Available at https://childtrauma.org/wp-content/uploads/2016/12/Sun-Interview-Bruce-Perry-Nov-2016.pdf (accessed 22/1/2019).

Sylvestre, A., Bussières, E-L. and Bouchard, C. (2016) 'Language problems among abused and neglected children: A meta-analytic review.' *Child Maltreatment, 21*, 1, 47–58.

Think U Know, n.d. *Keeping adopted children safe online.* Available at https://www.thinkuknow.co.uk/parents/articles/Young-peoples-use-of-the-internet-Advice-for-adoptive-parents (accessed 17/06/2018).

Tough, P. (2012) *How Children Succeed: Grit, Curiosity, and the Hidden Power of Character.* Mariner Books.

Tyborowskaa, A., Volman, I., Niermann, H.C.M, Pouwels, J.L., *et al.* (2018) 'Early-life and pubertal stress differentially modulate grey matter development in human adolescents.' *Scientific Reports*, June.

van der Kolk, B.A. (2014) *The Body Keeps the Score – Mind, Brain and Body in the Transformation of Trauma.* London: Allen Lane/Penguin Books.

World Health Organisation (2018) *International statistical classification of diseases and related health problems* (11th revision).

Further Resources

Helpful books for teachers and school staff

Inside I'm Hurting: Practical Strategies for Children with Attachment Difficulties in Schools by Louise Bombèr (2007)

What About Me? Inclusive Strategies to Support Pupils with Attachment Difficulties Make it Through the School Day by Louise Bombèr (2010)

Becoming an Adoption-Friendly School by Dr Emma Gore Langton and Katherine Boy (2017)

When the Adults Change, Everything Changes by Paul Dix (2017)

The Teacher's Introduction to Attachment: Practical Essentials for Teachers, Carers and School Support Staff by Nicola Marshall (2014)

Making a Difference: A Practical Guide for the Emotionally Focused School Practitioner by Cath Hunter (2018)

Better Behaviour: A Guide for Teachers by Jarlath O'Brien (2018)

Wider interest books

The Boy Who Was Raised as a Dog, by Bruce D. Perry (2006)

The Unofficial Guide to Adoptive Parenting: The Small Stuff, The Big Stuff and The Stuff In Between by Sally Donovan (2014)

A Therapeutic Treasure Box for Working with Children and Adolescents with Developmental Trauma: Creative Techniques and Activities by Karen Treisman (2017)

The A–Z of Therapeutic Parenting: Strategies and Solutions by Sarah Naish (2018)

Why Can't My Child Behave? Empathic Parenting Strategies That Work for Adoptive and Foster Families by Amber Elliott (2013)

Everyday Parenting with Security and Love: Using PACE to Provide Foundations for Attachment by Kim S. Golding (2017)

Connective Parenting: A Guide to Connecting With Your Child Using the NVR Approach by Sarah Fisher (2017)

Books for children

Rosie Rudey and the Very Annoying Parent (2016), *Charley Chatty and the Disappearing Pennies* (2017), *William Wobbly and the Very Bad Day* (2016) plus many others in this excellent series by Sarah Naish

The Boy Who Built a Wall Around Himself (2015) and *The Mermaid Who Couldn't: How Mariana Overcame Shame and Learned to Sing Her Own Song* by Ali Redford (2018)

Billy Bramble and the Great Big Cook Off by Sally Donovan (2016)

Online resources

Adoption UK – A selection of free education resources is available on their website here: www.adoptionuk.org/Pages/Category/education-resources. Adoption UK also offers schools membership to all schools across the UK.

PAC-UK – Free education resources are available to download here: www.pac-uk.org/our-services/education.

Beacon House – This therapeutic services provider offers a range of free resources, including videos, articles and visual resources that are useful for individuals, or as part of training within school: https://beaconhouse.org.uk/useful-resources.

Inner World Work – Highly visual free material for parents and educators, including the 'Whole Class Happy Pack': www.innerworldwork.co.uk/?page_id=45.

Subject Index

Author Index